'It is always good to see a first rate book being re-published and so not lost to a new generation. The whole matter of relating the gospel to a pagan culture is even more pressing than when Ken Prior first wrote this book. It has first rate academic integrity but also great practical challenge. Such a book is well worth a second airing.'

Philip H Hacking
July 1995

Christians often assume that evangelism is either about filling a vacuum or calling people from nominalism to a personal faith in Christ. Nothing could be further from the truth, for the most part the evangelist is addressing neither the nominal and not even post-Christian man but the modern pagan. Whether they are encountered in the market-place or on the door-step people of this present generation do have a belief system, albeit non-Christian. Sometimes it is vaguely articulated like the 'unknown god' of Athens, or at other times it may be more clearly articulated as the deity of a new age. Unless the evangelist is aware of this he will be missing the mark.

Ken Prior helps us to get the aim right by looking at how the apostle Paul spoke to the most sophisticated pagans of his day. This book is written out of the author's long experience in pastoral and evangelistic ministry. It contains a wealth of wisdom and clear thinking. I recommend it to anyone who wants to present the gospel in a way that challenges the modern pagan.

Rev James McAllen
London City Mission
June 1995

The Gospel in a Pagan Society

Kenneth Prior

CHRISTIAN FOCUS PUBLICATIONS

© 1995 Kenneth Prior
ISBN 1-85792-142-9

Published by
Christian Focus Publications Ltd.
Geanies House, Fearn, Ross-shire,
IV20 1TW, Scotland, Great Britain.

Printed and bound in Great Britain
by Cox & Wyman Ltd, Reading, Berkshire

Cover design by Donna Macleod

CONTENTS

FOREWORD

We live in a world where truth is rapidly becoming a neglected commodity. The appeal of advertising, propaganda and political pronouncements is to our own self-interest, and we recognise that each must be taken with a liberal 'dose of salt'.

For our postmodernist society has decided that all attempts by one person to share truth with another can never rise above the level of transmitting propaganda. Each individual is regarded as being entitled to their own opinions, but no-one possesses the right to inflict their ideas on another.

Once the Church was assumed to be in possession of the authority to dictate what was, or was not, the truth – and this could be imposed on all people. Then came the eighteenth century 'Enlightenment', and human reason replaced the Church as the ultimate arbiter of truth. This 'modernity' which denied that truth could ever be unreasonable to the human mind attained its final peak in the mid-1950s, subsequent decades saw it collapse before the onslaught of postmodernist thinking.

Today this view is disseminated through the soap-opera, tabloid press and the overwhelming weight of popular opinion. No longer is the principle of absolute truth accepted. All truth is relative, so homosexual practice, cohabitation and abortion have become a matter of personal opinion – what is right for one person cannot be assumed to be the same for another.

Not only is this philosophy applied to moral values but also to religious beliefs. All roads are viewed as leading to the same destination, every religion is intrinsically identical, each is an equally effective route to God. The multiplication of inter-faith services is regarded with popular approval.

Tragically, the response of many evangelical Christians to this phenomena has been one of withdrawal rather than engagement. We readily conclude that society is something from which we must be separate, that social and religious aberrations are inevitable (and cannot be changed by us), that even a response to these trends might somehow compromise our stand for truth.

The Apostle Paul did not adopt this position. He was prepared to engage with people at Athens from where their attitudes were, not where he wanted them to be. That is why this new edition of Canon Kenneth Prior's significant work is both relevant and appropriate. For it engages plurality of gods in Athens with the Biblical proclamation of the Apostle, and it would be difficult to find a model which is more applicable to the pluralism of today's world.

When confronted with a similar challenge from society it is so inadequate to simply exclaim,

'You ask me how I know He lives,
He lives within my heart.'

We need to follow the Biblical urging to 'give a reason for the faith that is within us'.

A postmodernist outlook is perfectly willing to accept our testimony, alongside that of everyone else – what it is unable to do is to recognise that what we share is true for others as well as ourselves. It fails to recognise 'true truth', and accepts that each can worship an 'unknown god' suitable for themselves.

The vague response of a woolly-minded humanism has been to affirm, along with Anne Diamond, that – 'it doesn't matter what you believe, just so long as you are sincere about it'. Too often the Church has failed to express the fact that such a view is simply wrong.

Paul delivered that verdict. He did not apply it with condemnation of their ignorance but with warm commendation of the Lord Jesus. That same mixture of serious conviction with compassionate concern resonates through the pages of Ken Prior's book.

It is time for us to abandon the arid deserts of spiritual neutrality and to face up to the issues of our day. It is impossible to achieve this desire without returning to Scripture. Ken Prior makes us do both. The longing of his heart is clearly that non-Christians might meet Jesus. His commitment goes further in extending the desire that Christians may be re-energised to fulfil their Biblical obligation, and to witness to the truth that alone is found in Jesus Christ.

Back to the Bible. Such is the thesis of this book which maintains that Scripture still has the answers for today. It therefore repays careful study by all who want to provide a clear reply to the postmodernist worldview of so many in contemporary society. For only then will we be able to adequately communicate the relevance of the changeless Word to a changing world – and that we must do, for the sake of our King, and His Kingdom.

Clive Calver
London, June, 1995

PREFACE

Rewriting a book which was published twenty years ago calls for some explanation. Its origin was even longer ago in a series of lectures I gave to a conference of theological students. The reason is simply that I have received a number of requests from both sides of the Atlantic, either for now unobtainable copies of the original, or that I should produce a revised edition. And the reason in every case is the same: *the book is considered to be even more relevant now than when it first appeared.*

The predominant evangelistic method which our generation has inherited has been to invite unbelievers to religious meetings, whether the large rally originally given prominence in Victorian times by Moody and Sankey, or smaller local gatherings such as guest services and parish missions. That has worked well in reaching nominal Christians and others who share some of our presuppositions. But as Western society departs further from its Christian heritage, and becomes increasingly pagan, we are compelled to ask whether we need to think again about our approach.

Many books have been written which purport to analyse the situation. Some point to the latest success story, which always receives a good press and encourage others to try to transplant it elsewhere. So often, however, impressive statistics in evangelism are found where the people reached have some kind of Christian background. This book faces the challenge of a society where there is no such background. And there is nothing new in this. Not only is it what every pioneer missionary has had to face, but it is the kind of setting in which the gospel first spread across the world in New Testament times under the leadership of the first great missionary-evangelist, the apostle Paul. It is of utmost importance then, that in our discussions about the presentation of the gospel today, we take into account the manner in which the Apostle to the Gentiles set about preaching the gospel to the pagan society of his day, and do not waste any of the lessons he left on record.

It seems that Luke selected for special treatment Paul's time in Athens, because it is an example of his approach in what was the cultural centre of the pagan world of the first century. We are given not only a brief account with significant details of Paul's encounter in the market place with the ordinary people of Athens, but also his own explanation of this ministry for the benefit of the intelligentsia of Athens and hopefully for our benefit also. Even a hurried reading of it shows how different is Paul's approach from what has been the typical evangelistic meeting which has come to be the accepted style.

I have for a long time assumed that the 'Areopagus address' as we have it in Acts 17 is not a complete transcript of all that Paul said, but consists of the notes which Luke obtained from him. If you read Paul's address aloud you will find that at the most it

takes two minutes, and even to stretch it out to this
time you will have to read it fairly slowly. Now no
one will ever convince me that the great apostle ever
gave an address which lasted only two minutes! So
presumably we have the main outline of what Paul
said expressed, no doubt, in some of the striking
phrases which impressed themselves on Luke's mind.
And what suggestive points they are! Luke's account
gives us a clear idea of Paul's approach, his main
emphases, the conclusions he drew and the applica-
tions he made.

I am not suggesting that Paul's world was in every
way that matters identical with ours, nor that the way
of success lies in a slavish following of him in every
detail. There are differences between pre-Christian
paganism which Paul encountered in Athens and the
post-Christian paganism of today. But we can learn
valuable lessons from these also, if the way in which
Paul adapted himself and applied his message to the
people of his day, helps us to do the same for the
people of ours.

There is an alternative appraisal of Paul's policy
in Athens which we cannot ignore. It is the suggestion that his entire approach was a mistake and that
he himself had later misgivings. This is a view which,
though understandable, I cannot accept, but we shall
not be in a position to consider it until we have com-
pleted our study. We shall not confine ourselves to
the Areopagus address itself, but will look first at
the account given in the preceding verses of Paul's
witness in Athens over several days. Some misun-

derstandings of the Areopagus address have arisen
out of overlooking the fact that it is Paul's own explanation of the significance of his activities in the
market place in answer to the questions put to him.

My aim in revising this book, as with the first
edition, is not to present any bright ideas of my own
on evangelism. Of such I have few or none. It is to
attempt to set out the way that Paul tackled an alien
scene in his day with the hope and prayer that it will
shed some light on how to tackle the challenge before us today. I suggest that there is much material
here to contribute to discussions on evangelism, and
I daresay that those better qualified than I will have
suggestions as to how to apply it.

Paul in Athens
(Acts 17:13-34)

When the Jews in Thessalonica learned that Paul was preaching the word of God at Berea, they went there too, agitating the crowds and stirring them up. The brothers immediately sent Paul to the coast, but Silas and Timothy stayed at Berea. The men who escorted Paul brought him to Athens and then left with instructions for Silas and Timothy to join him as soon as possible.

While Paul was waiting for them in Athens, he was greatly distressed to see that the city was full of idols. So he reasoned in the synagogue with the Jews and the God-fearing Greeks, as well as in the market-place day by day with those who happened to be there. A group of Epicurean and Stoic philosophers began to dispute with him. Some of them asked, 'What is this babbler trying to say?' Others remarked, 'He seems to be advocating foreign gods.' They said this because Paul was preaching the good news about Jesus and the resurrection. Then they took him and brought him to a meeting of the Areopagus, where they said to him, 'May we know what this new teaching is that you are presenting? You are bringing some strange ideas to our ears, and we want to know what they mean.' (All the Athenians and the foreigners who lived there spent their time doing nothing but talking about and listening to the latest ideas.)

Paul then stood up in the meeting of the Areopagus and said: 'Men of Athens! I see that in every way you are very religious. For as I walked around and looked carefully at your objects of worship, I even found an altar with this inscription: TO AN UNKNOWN god. Now what you worship as something unknown I am going to proclaim to you.

'The God who made the world and everything in it is the Lord of heaven and earth and does not live in temples built by hands. And he is not served by human hands, as if he needed anything, because he himself gives all men life and breath and everything else. From one man he made every nation of men, that they should inhabit the whole earth; and he determined the times set for them and the exact places where they should live. God did this so that men would seek him and perhaps reach out for him and find him, though he is not far from each one of us. "For in him we live and move and have our being." As some of your own poets have said, "We are his offspring."

'Therefore since we are God's offspring, we should not think that the divine being is like gold or silver or stone – an image made by man's design and skill. In the past God overlooked such ignorance, but now he commands all people everywhere to repent. For he has set a day when he will judge the world with justice by the man he has appointed. He has given proof of this to all men by raising him from the dead.'

When they heard about the resurrection of the dead, some of them sneered, but others said, 'We want to hear you again on this subject.' At that, Paul left the Council. A few men became followers of Paul and believed. Among them was Dionysius, a member of the Areopagus, also a woman named Damaris, and a number of others.

1

SOWING OR REAPING

A well-known evangelist's efforts in a particular
place have been described as 'having apparently
made little impression'. Admittedly this is part of
an amplified version of the original report, but it
fairly reflects the results as estimated by the evangelist's own henchman. The evangelist was none
other than the apostle Paul, and the description is
from J. B. Phillips' expanded version of Luke's account, which is included at the end of *The Young
Church in Action*. As you have probably guessed,
the occasion was Paul's visit to Athens. To quote
Luke more literally, 'A few men became followers
of Paul and believed', while at the same time he
records the response of others who said, 'We want
to hear you again on this subject' (Acts 17:32,34).
That summarises the results of Paul's time in Athens.

It would seem that this was not the only occasion when Paul had only a little to show for his
evangelistic efforts. A study of the New Testament
records shows that the way was often hard and
progress slow. There were times when Paul, human
as he was, needed to be encouraged out of a feeling
of failure and disappointment.[1] Many of the

churches immediately resulting from his preaching were not all that large, even by today's often depressing standards. Yet it was from these small beginnings that the Church of Jesus Christ took root and grew. That is what happened in Athens because by the early part of the second century there was a flourishing church there.

How are we to estimate the result of Paul's mission to Athens? It would not look well among the statistics of many present-day evangelistic efforts. Nor does it compare too well with what happened in Jerusalem on the Day of Pentecost and the weeks that followed. It is sometimes assumed that the impressive results of those days were entirely due to the power of the Holy Spirit, whereby the Apostles were able to carry all before them with a constant torrent of converts pouring into the church. If only we could in some way have a repetition of the experience of Pentecost, so it is said, the same results would follow.

Now the last thing we want to do is to detract in any way from what God did on the Day of Pentecost. Nor do we want to discourage any Christian from ensuring that he does not fall short of anything that God has made available through the operation of his Spirit. At the same time, however, we must not imagine that in New Testament times success, on the scale that they knew it at Pentecost and in the days immediately following, attended their preaching all the time. Later, when we leave Jerusalem and its surroundings and watch Paul on his missionary journeys, the picture is somewhat different.

Why should this be? Was it that Paul's experience of the Holy Spirit fell short of those who laboured with such success in Jerusalem? This is the explanation that is sometimes advanced for lack of success in evangelism today. I should like to have heard Paul's answer if this explanation were applied to him!

The answer is surely that evangelism can be one of two forms. All true evangelism would be covered by what has long been a standard definition:

> To evangelise is so to present Christ Jesus in the power of the Holy Spirit, that men shall come to put their trust in God through him, to accept him as their Saviour, and serve him as their King in the fellowship of his Church.[2]

When we come to describe the actual work of evangelism, or the distinctive task of someone specially called to be an evangelist, it has be defined in two different ways. Some speak of it as sowing, while others conceive of it as reaping. Failure to recognise these two alternative definitions can cause confusion and lead to talking at cross purposes. We begin with the second of them – reaping.

Several years ago I attended a very helpful conference on evangelism. One of its purposes was to promote understanding between those engaged in full-time evangelism and pastors of local churches. I well remember the contribution of a full-time evangelist who had also spent some years in pastoral ministry. The pastor, he explained, sowed the seed, usually over a long period of time. Then, at the opportune moment, it is the turn of the evangelist to be called in and reap what has been sown. In this way the faithful work of the pastor finds fruition, and so the two kinds of ministry are complementary to each other. He went on to offer another metaphor likening the evangelist to a midwife. After a period of gestation he is sent for and the converts are brought to the birth. The essential gift of the evangelist in this sense is the ability to 'bring people to decision'. This has often involved the use of certain techniques (pardon the word) such as inviting new converts to stand up, raise their hands or 'come forward' as an outward declaration of their decision.

It is necessary to recognise the assumption underlying this conception of the work of an evangelist. It is the recognition that the potential convert already has some kind of Christian background to which the evangelist can appeal. It may be the result of a pastor's work, Christian teaching at day school, or Sunday School during childhood. There has undoubtedly been much successful evangelism of this kind over the past hundred years or so. It has ensured that those within a Christian tradition, when it may often have been comparatively easy to be a nominal Christian, are challenged to make a real commitment to Christ. Sankey and Moody and their successors have been very effective in this type of evangelism. Evangelism in British Universities used to owe a great deal to Christian principles, previously learned in public schools and daily worship in their chapels, even though the latter have not usually been noted for evangelical fervour!

I had experience of this during twelve years of continuing evangelism in a London church, where a constantly changing population meant that we came into contact with a large number and wide range of people. Among the many who professed conversion at guest services and other evangelistic gatherings, the majority had some kind of Christian background whether through church, home or school. Many of them would have called themselves Christians, even though they had never really understood what commitment to Christ really meant. It was often something of a shock when they encountered evangelical Christianity either through preaching or in the lives and witness of their Christian friends. So the account of their conversion would often run like this: 'I thought I was a Christian until I met ...' All they needed was to encounter what a real Christian is without any need to argue that it is true. In those days many non-churchgoers would claim to be Christian, adding that they were as good as any who went to church.

There will always be a place for this type of evangelism as long as there are nominal Christians. Churches which take their evangelistic responsibilities seriously will usually have organisations which befriend outsiders and build up a fringe membership. Through such contact with the church the seed of God's word is gradually being sown in their hearts, and the time will come for them to respond in repentance and faith. What has been sown will then be reaped.

Now all this is basically the kind of evangelism we read of in the early chapters of Acts. What happened on the Day of Pentecost is typical. Those who heard the apostles and from whom the three thousand converts were drawn were certainly not pagans. Many of them were Jews who lived in Jerusalem and its immediate vicinity. Others were Jews of the Dispersion who lived in other parts of the world, but who cared enough to come up to Jerusalem for the Feast of Pentecost. A third group represented were not Jews by race, but Gentiles who had been convinced of the value of the Jewish religion, in many cases through the enthusiastic proselytising activity of the Jews, and had come to embrace it for themselves. The people in Jerusalem that day, as Luke summarises it, included, 'both Jews and converts to Judaism, Cretans and Arabs' (Acts 2:11).

What all these people held in common was their Old Testament background, with its high moral principles such as the Ten Commandments, expectations of a coming Messiah and, above all, a lofty conception of the being and character of God. This clearly determined Peter's approach to them, evidenced as it is by his quotations from the prophet Joel and the Psalms. In particular, he assumed that when he claimed that God has made Jesus 'both Lord and

Christ' (Acts 2:36) they would know what he was talking about.

The results of evangelism on ground prepared by Old Testament teaching were impressive. The small handful of disciples that emerged from the upper room on the Day of Pentecost found themselves suddenly augmented by the addition of 'about three thousand' (Acts 2:41). During the days that followed church expansion continued as 'the Lord added to their number daily those who were being saved'. Two chapters later Luke records that 'many who heard the message believed, and the number of men grew to about five thousand' (Acts 4:4). Chapter six opens with the disciples still increasing, and then summarises progress:

> So the word of God spread. The number of disciples in Jerusalem increased rapidly, and a large number of priests became obedient to the faith (Acts 6:7).

Note, however, that all this was *in Jerusalem* where for centuries prophet and priest had sown God's truth, and where the New Testament preachers were now reaping with such outstanding effectiveness. Is this quite the same as evangelising those with a Christian background? Perhaps not entirely, although the basic attitude maintained by a first-century Jew is by no means dissimilar to the respectability of many a nominal Christian today. There are also examples of evangelism within the churches of the New Testament. Was it not to people Paul addressed as 'the church of God in Corinth' that he appealed 'be reconciled to God'? (2 Cor. 5:20). And at the end of that same epistle he revealed his doubts about some of his readers in the advice, 'examine yourselves to see whether you are in the faith; test yourselves' (2 Cor. 13:5). So we shall continue to proclaim the gospel in our churches while they contain those lacking a personal commitment to Christ. As long as there are non-Christians who to some degree acknowledge the church, we shall invite them to our guest services and other means geared to reach them.

Our prime concern in this book, however, is with those with no Christian background, and who share few if any of our presuppositions. They may still attend a church for the occasional funeral or wedding, because they have friends with varying degrees of church connection, but at no other times, not even Christmas or Easter. Many of a previous generation excused their lack of church attendance because they did their bit when they were children, when they were forced to attend three times on a Sunday. We now have a generation without any childhood involvement in a church and with an almost complete ignorance of the most basic points of the Christian Faith. Although many of previous generations seldom went to church, they still held to Christian morality and expected this would earn them a place in heaven. That has all changed and Christian moral standards can never be taken for granted. Back in 1969 Francis Schaeffer described this change in society as follows:

In the United States in the short span from the twenties to the sixties we have seen a complete shift. Of course not every one in the United States in the twenties was a Christian, but in general there was a Christian consensus. Now that consensus has completely gone. Ours is a post Christian world in which Christianity, not only in the number of Christians but in cultural emphasis and in cultural result, is now in the absolute minority. To ask people to maintain the status quo is folly. The status quo in no longer ours .... When we begin to think of them and preach the gospel to them, we must begin with the fact that they have no knowledge of biblical Christianity. But it is more than this, for the whole culture has shifted from Christian to post-Christian.[3]

A further feature of most Western countries is a multi-racial population containing substantial minorities brought up in non-Christian religions. Hindu and Sikh temples and Moslem mosques are now a common sight in many of our cities.

This is in all essentials the situation faced by the preachers of the gospel in the first century. Once they travelled outside Palestine, they found themselves in a pluralist society quite ignorant of the God revealed in Scripture. In morals it was a society as permissive as today's and there was little to uplift them in any of the pagan religions on offer. It was only in the small Jewish communities that existed in many of the cities, that they found those who shared their presuppositions. Sometimes they were large enough for a synagogue to be formed. Very often, as at Philippi, only a handful of women would meet to pray (Acts 16:13).

How can you describe an evangelist in such a situation? As a reaper, reaping where others have sown? Hardly. He is now a pioneer, breaking completely fresh ground. And this was Paul's ministry the moment he said at Antioch in Pisidia, 'we now turn to the Gentiles' (Acts 13:46). It is true that when he arrived in a new city he usually made the synagogue his first point of contact, but he regarded himself first and foremost as 'the apostle to the Gentiles' (Rom. 11:13), and his call to this ministry he traced right back to the beginning of his Christian experience (Acts 22:21).

This ministry had many differences from that among the Jews and their Gentile proselytes. In particular progress was far slower. Paul had his successes among the Gentiles, it is true. In addition to those who attended the synagogues and responded in large numbers when Paul preached in them (e.g. Iconium – Acts 14:1) there was encouragement at Derbe where he and Barnabas 'won a large number of disciples' (Acts 14:21), and again at the beginning of the second missionary journey (Acts 16:5). Yet we cannot fail to notice that there are no examples of converts being numbered in thousands as they had known in Jerusalem and district at Pentecost and the days immediately following. Sometimes results among complete pagans were quite small, as Paul found at Athens. So we are bound to agree with the observation of Michael Green:

The Christian faith grew fastest and best on Jewish soil, or at least on soil which had been prepared by Judaism. [4]

Yet in spite of its difficulties and slowness in showing results, Paul gloried in pioneer evangelism, which involved sowing the seed of the gospel in virgin soil, and he made it the dominant aim of his life. Here is how he described this ministry:

It has always been my ambition to preach the gospel where Christ was not known, so that I would not be building on someone else's foundation. Rather, as it is written: 'Those who were not told about him will see, and those who have not heard will understand' (Rom. 15:20-21).

In another passage he confesses that this is a privilege which leaves him with a sense of complete unworthiness:

Although I am less than the least of all of God's people, this grace was given me: to preach to the Gentiles the unsearchable riches of Christ (Eph. 3:8).

Such an attitude enabled Paul to persevere when the task was uphill and discouraging. Even when he was about to explain the spiritual blindness of many of his hearers as satanic in origin, he still claimed, 'Therefore, since through God's mercy we have this ministry, we do not lose heart' (2 Cor. 4:1).

We have to recognise that this conception of an evangelist as a sower and pioneer rather than a reaper has not been the dominant one since Victorian times. In 1968 the British Evangelical Alliance set up a commission on evangelism and the subsequent report included the following observation:

> Over the last one hundred years this function has been increasingly exercised in a way which has emphasised the public rather than the personal, and reaping rather than sowing.[5]

In the years which have since passed, it has become increasingly clear that this will do no longer. We need to recapture something of the apostle's sense of thrill at the prospect of pioneer evangelism, even if it means ceasing to rely for our satisfaction on results which show impressive statistics. When Western society was more Christian than it is today, this was largely reserved for overseas missionaries. Many a Christian at home found the romance of their lives irresistible, even if the response to the missionary call never went beyond the realms of fantasy. Today we do not have to cross the sea to be surrounded by Hindu temples, Moslem mosques or Chinese pagodas to be missionary pioneers. Right where we are we are among people 'where Christ was not known'. So while we shall not neglect the so-called religious people who need the gospel ('to the Jew first' as Paul would have put it), an increasing number of us must share his 'ambition to preach the gospel where Christ was not known' (Romans 15:20).

2

ART FORMS AND IDOLS

If Luke wanted to choose an example of how Paul approached the pagan world of his day with the gospel, he could not have chosen a better example than Paul's visit to Athens, for it was its cultural capital. It was noted for philosophy with illustrious names like Socrates, Plato and Aristotle among its thinkers. It also boasted great literature and dramatic art with the plays of the celebrated trio, Aeschylus, Sophocles and Euripides. But what first attracted Paul's attention was its architecture and sculpture of which there was much to see, as is still the case today. While Paul awaited the arrival of his companions, Silas and Timothy, whom he had left behind in Thessalonica, he decided to fill in the time with a sightseeing tour. What he saw affected him deeply:

> While Paul was waiting for them in Athens, he was greatly distressed to see that the city was full of idols (Acts 17:16).

We know from the ruins still standing today, and from exhibits in our museums, that Athens abounded in works of art, the most prominent being the Parthenon which can be seen from a long way around. What we don't always remember is their religious

31

significance, and that so many of them were, in fact, idols. To New Testament Christians like Paul this mattered much more than any artistic merit they may have possessed, even though, with his education, he was by no means uncultured. As Professor Blaiklock in a Rendle Short memorial lecture pointed out:

> Those who view with wonder the magnificence of Athens' ruined heart today, are without the Jews' deep loathing of idolatry.[1]

This was the attitude in which Paul had been nurtured. Not only did the Law of God forbid the worship of other gods, as the first of the Ten Commandments made clear, but Jehovah himself was not to be worshipped in an idolatrous fashion either. This was forbidden in the second of the Commandments. What God's Law commanded, the prophets of Israel constantly preached to a people that found it all too easy to fall in with the idolatrous practices of the surrounding tribes. Not that they necessarily worshipped pagan deities, as they did in the Northern Kingdom during the reign of Ahab through the influence of his queen, Jezebel, a heathen princess, who imported her own native Baal, Melqart, together with hundreds of his prophets. Often they thought they could maintain the religion of Jehovah by compromising it with idolatry, when they represented him by a metal bull which they set up at the high places, together with the degrading practices associated with it. So even when Baal worship was banned by the better kings, the following proviso had sometimes to be added:

'The high places, however, were not removed, and the people continued to offer sacrifices and burn incense there.' [2]

The time came, however, when the battle against idolatry was decisively won, and the people learned once and for all the lesson that generations of prophets had tried to bring home to them. That happened during the Babylonian exile, and when they returned to their own land, it was as a people purified from the defilement of idolatry. It was just as one of the prophets of the exile said it would be:

> For I will take you out of the nations; I will gather you from all the countries and bring you back into your own land. I will sprinkle clean water on you, and you will be clean; I will cleanse you from all your impurities and *from all your idols* (Ezekiel 36:24-25).

The post-exilic Jews certainly had their faults, but idolatry wasn't one of them. They had learnt their lesson the hard way and it would never be forgotten.

This was the attitude inherited by the New Testament Christians from their immediate Jewish predecessors, and which they took with them as they evangelised in the Greek cities. Turning from idolatry was expected by the apostles of their converts. This was made clear in the message sent to Gentile converts from the Council of Jerusalem in Acts 15. Circumcision would not be required of them, but they were expected, among other things, to have nothing to do with idolatry. This was one of the most obvious ways in which someone converted out of paganism would give evidence of his repentance. It was in such terms that Paul reminded the Thessalonians of their conversion: '... how you turned to God from idols to serve the living and true God' (1 Thess. 1:9).

When we come to Acts 17 it is perhaps of some significance that Luke uses an Old Testament word to describe Paul's reaction to the idolatry of Athens. The word translated 'greatly distressed' (NIV) and 'provoked' (RSV) is the one used in the Septuagint of Jehovah being provoked to anger by idolatry. And the reason for God's reaction to idolatry was always the same: he could not tolerate anything which detracts from the honour due to his own name, whether it be rival deities, or representing himself in an unworthy fashion. As he asserts through Isaiah:

> I am the LORD; that is my name! I will not give my glory to another or my praise to idols (Isaiah 42:8).

The Old Testament often refers to God's reaction to idols as jealousy. It is like the perfectly justifiable jealousy of a married person over adulterous behaviour on the part of the spouse.

So the uncompromising stand of the early Christians against idolatry was not out of disapproval of art for which they could make no appeal to the Old Testament. No less a person than Moses, who had been given the task of delivering God's commandments, including those concerned with idolatry, was at the same time involved with much art work in the Tabernacle. The curtains, for example, were adorned with embroidered figures, there were the cherubim overshadowing the Ark of the Covenant and the golden candlesticks in the form of a tree. The artistic gifts of Bezalel which were fully used in embellishing the Tabernacle, and which ensured him a place in Old Testament history, are attributed to being 'filled with the Spirit of God' (Exod. 35:31). Solomon's Temple, which later replaced the Tabernacle, was no less adorned. We read of Solomon that

> On all the walls around the temple, in both the inner and outer rooms, he carved cherubim, palm trees and open flowers (1 Kings 6:29).

Idols, however, had a significance of their own. They were pathetic rivals to Jehovah, the living God. And they did not have to take the form of inanimate objects. All forms of polytheism were equally obnoxious. Paul met an example of this at Lystra where, to make matters worse, he and his colleague Barnabas themselves became the objects of idolatry by a crowd that had been carried away with unthinking enthusiasm by the spectacle of Paul healing a cripple. It is little wonder that Paul recoiled in horror exclaiming:

> Men, why are you doing this? We too are only men, human like you. We are bringing you good news, telling you to turn from these worthless things to the living God, who made heaven and earth ... (Acts 14:15).

Just as Old Testament prophets saw them as rivals to Jehovah, so New Testament apostles, jealous for the glory of Jesus Christ, could not tolerate any rivals

either. To them the truth 'Jesus is Lord' lay at the
very heart of what they believed and lived for, and
was a dignity he could share with no other. So they
had to make their position regarding idolatry unmis-
takably plain. As Michael Green has explained,

> It would be pointless to preach Jesus as Lord if he
> were merely to be thought of as an addition to an al-
> ready overcrowded pantheon.[3]

Indeed Paul's experience in Athens provides a clear
example of this very danger. Whether it was through
difficulties of language o dialect it is impossible to
tell, but some of Paul's hearers got the idea that he
was offering them two extra deities, 'Jesus and the
Resurrection' (Acts 17:18).

One of the chief points the Old Testament makes
about the making of images is to draw attention to
its futility. All that idolaters succeed in doing is 'worshipping what their hands have made' (Jer. 1:16). In
Isaiah's classical passages on this subject the language becomes quite derisory (e.g. Isa. 2:8; 14:18-
20). Having described the skill and ingenuity with
which the craftsman makes his idol, Isaiah observes
how 'he bows down to it and worships. He prays to it
and says, "Save me; you are my god" ' (Isa. 44:17).
A few lines later the voice of God comes in with the
salutary reminder: 'Remember these things, O Jacob,
for you are my servant, O Israel. I have made you,
you are my servant' (Isa. 44:21).

What has all this to do with presenting the gospel
today? After all we would hardly suspect anyone to-

day in a civilised society of having a totem pole in their back garden to dance around on special family occasions. But before we swallow the assumption that the worship of idols is beneath sophisticated twenti-eth-century minds, we ought to appreciate that idols do not have to be physical objects. It is just as possi-ble to have idols in our minds as we create mental images of the kind of God we like to conceive. When we substitute 'image' for idol we have the main root of the word 'imagination'. This is the very thing that people do when they introduce their idea of God with expressions such as 'I like to think ...'. It is of-ten used to invent an easy-going God, whose love is presumed to preclude him from punishing sin. Or we think of him as an old man with a beard. In this way we can create a god who is far removed from the God who made himself known through Christ and the Bible.

Sometimes the God we invent fits in with the passing fashions of contemporary thought. This was what lay at the root of idolatry in the Old Testament. It meant that Israel compromised their understand-ing of God which had been revealed to them with the popular ideas of the surrounding pagan tribes. The danger is just the same with us today. There seem to be grounds for saying that this was what John Robinson was doing in his book *Honest to God* which caused a great stir when it was published in 1963. Anyway that was the assessment of J. I. Packer who entitled his critique of John Robinson's views *Keep Yourselves From Idols*.

The trouble is that when we invent our own ideas of God, we simply create him in our own image, whereas the truth is the opposite – we have been created in God's image. Because of this the gods and goddesses of ancient Greece and Rome were no more than enlarged human beings. They were regarded as heads of department with gods of love, war, travel and so on. Worse than that, men have even projected their sins on to the gods of their own making. It has been said that if the gods and goddesses of ancient Greece were alive today, most of them would be in prison!

There has, however, been no need for Jewish and Christian people, with God revealed to them through the Bible, to resort to their own imaginings. Nor should we attempt to represent him by any physical shape. The Bible asks of the God it reveals, 'To whom then will you compare God? What image will you compare him to?' (Isa. 40:18). Simply to ask such a question excludes the possibility of idolatry. John Eddison has suggested that it is like 'trying to reproduce a painting by Constable on a blackboard, or do justice to a Beethoven symphony on a mouth organ'.[4]

Furthermore, just as men are not to represent God in this way, he has not chosen to reveal himself in this way either. This is very clear from God's method of self-disclosure in the Old Testament, as R. W. Dale once observed:

God wished to be thought of by the Jews as he had revealed himself in his words and acts .... Throughout

their history he sent them - not painters or sculptors –
but prophets.[5]

When he did eventually reveal himself visibly it was
in the person of Christ. Then, instead of the distor-
tions of idolatry, whether in metal or stone or just in
the imagination, John could write, 'We have seen his
glory, the glory of the One and Only, who came from
the Father, full of grace and truth' (John 1:14).

There is yet a further reason why, presumably, Paul
reacted in the way that he did to the idols of Athens.
Idolatry had long been associated with gross forms
of sexual immorality and perversion. Paul lays considerable stress on this in the first chapter of his letter to the Romans. The degrading practices he mentions are seen as a natural consequence of idolatry.
Here is how C. K. Barrett describes the connection
between the two:

> In the obscene pleasures to which he refers is to be
> seen precisely that perversion of the created order
> which may be expected when men put the creation in
> place of the Creator. [6]

This was particularly true of Canaanite religion in
which even the 'worship' itself involved sexual or-
gies, and the fertility cults were accompanied by practices of the most degrading kind. When heathen idolatry was imported into Israelite religion it brought
these corruptions with it. This is a telling example of
the way that belief and worship can affect conduct.

When Paul surveyed the scene in Athens he would

hardly have failed to observe that idolatry there had the same corrupt associations. There were some repulsive examples of which remnants can be seen today and of which E. M. Blaiklock has frankly written:

> Perhaps the Christian can still touch the edge of that deep sensation only in the revolting presence of the phallic image. Some fragments, vast and intricately carved on Delos, reveal the gross mingling of carnality and religion which stirred the wrath of the Hebrew prophets, and which evoke a Christian disgust. The sculptured sensualities of some Eastern temples stir the same nausea. Athens must have had examples enough of the baser use of Greek art. [7]

It is often said that art reflects, as it should, the outlook and spirit of its age. Paul knew that this was true of what was before him. Athens was just like most other cities of those days, full of corruption and vice. Because of their ignorance of God, as he told the Ephesians, 'having lost all sensitivity, they have given themselves over to sensuality so as to indulge in every kind of impurity, with a continual lust for more' (Eph. 4:19). And here in Athens were art forms that declared these tragic facts.

When Paul arrived in Athens, then, before he uttered a word to any of its people, Athens said something to him. The works of art which surrounded him were reminders that here were people in utter ignorance of God, whose only idea of him was limited to the distorted representations of the gods and goddesses of human imagination. Coupled with this was a way of life which underlined their lost condition.

Today we know only too well that art in the twentieth century conveys the same message. Its plays, films, novels and songs are constantly complaining of man's lost condition, as he struggles to find some meaning to life. Christians and other decent minded people are often appalled at the increasing amount of violence and obscenity being portrayed on stage and screen. But any suggestion of censorship is opposed by asserting not only the right, but also the duty to portray life as it truly is. In which case Paul's description quoted above is not very wide of the mark as a portrayal of moral standards today – not a pretty picture! And it is an admission of society's desperate spiritual condition.

Now what was Paul's response to this picture of the spiritual and moral life of Athens? As we have noticed 'he was greatly distressed'. The imperfect tense indicates that this was not restricted to the initial shock of what he saw, but it remained with him. In these days it is all too easy to become accustomed to the corruption and degradation of modern pagan society as we see it constantly portrayed on our television screens. We must never allow this to happen if we are to share in Paul's strong motivation to share the gospel with a world which so desperately needs it. Like Paul we shall be jealous for the glory of God and be deeply concerned at the way his name is blasphemed. It was with such concerns that Paul went out into Athens with just the gospel for such a pagan society.

3

IN THE MARKET-PLACE

The next verse in Luke's account shows us how Paul set about responding to the challenge which confronted him:

> So he reasoned in the synagogue with the Jews and God-fearing Greeks, as well as in the market-place day by day with those who happened to be there (Acts 17:17).

In keeping with his usual practice he made a start in the synagogue with the Jews, and with Gentiles who had been attracted to the Jewish religion. Although we are not supplied with any details, we can safely assume that he followed his usual approach when invited to speak. We have an example of this at the beginning of the same chapter, where Luke gives us a fair idea of the line Paul took in the synagogue at Thessalonica. He could assume an acceptance and some knowledge of Old Testament Scripture, so 'he reasoned with them from the Scriptures' (verse 2). His purpose was to demonstrate that those Scriptures anticipated that the Messiah (or 'Christ' to use the Greek equivalent of the Hebrew) would suffer and then rise from the dead, and that far from being a contradiction of Messiahship as the Jews assumed, 'the Christ had to suffer and rise from the dead' (verse 3). He then proceeded to identify the Christ of Old Testament expectation with Jesus whom he proclaimed (verse 3). Luke observes that this occupied Paul for three successive Sabbaths.

Now this approach is basically identical with that of Peter in Jerusalem on the Day of Pentecost, identifying Jesus in his death and resurrection with the Messiah of Old Testament expectation. Paul, like Peter, was reaping what had previously been sown as he appealed to Scripture for support of his points. To affirm the truth he simply had to show what 'The Bible says ...'. Also he was conducting this ministry in the context of prayer and worship in the place where Old Testament believers met for that purpose. Here are basic similarities to much of the reaping type of evangelism we have known during this century.

Out there in Athens, however, was a very different situation. So how did he set about reaching the population of Athens with the gospel? Surely the first simple point to stress is that he went out to where they were, in the market place and finishing up on Mars Hill. He did not organise an evangelistic service in the synagogue, and invite Athenians to come in, even supposing that the Jewish authorities had permitted it. Nor did he hand out song sheets with the Psalms and other Jewish or Christian poems and try to conduct the Athenians in praising God in whom they did not believe, using the latest hit tunes of Athens! (Why should Zeus have all the best music?) Still less did he ask them either in the market place or on Mars Hill to bow their heads for a word of prayer!

Now all this sounds obvious enough for first-century pagan Athens, but what about pagan America or Europe today? When I was a young man I was explaining to an older Christian (who happened to be a Baptist) why we in our church had the baptismal font at the back of the church building just inside the entrance. It is, I pointed out, to express the fact that baptism marks entrance into church membership. 'No,' he replied, assuming he had won an important point, 'before a person can be baptised he must sit in the pews where he can hear and respond to the gospel.' Although in the first century non-Christians would not normally be expected to attend church before they were converted, many of my generation inherited the assumption that they would. The way of evangelism, as often as not, would be to invite our friends and neighbours to attend church and sit on pews where they would hear the gospel. Sometimes special efforts would be made by holding evangelistic missions or single 'guest services'. There our non-Christian friends would be led in prayer, expected to praise God by joining in Christian hymns and even contribute to the offertory when the plate was passed round!

It was, of course, often recognized that a church was not the best building to which to invite people, so evangelistic meetings would take place on 'neutral' ground, such as a town hall, concert hall or tent. But it was still to be fed with the same diet of prayers and hymns. Indeed some have felt such a content to be essential. Many years ago I addressed an evangelistic gathering in a hotel lounge. There were many unbelievers present and we had a useful time. I shall always remember how a Christian expressed deep concern that there had been no prayer during the course of the meeting. Happily he immediately saw the point when I assured him that some of us had prayed together before the meeting began, and asked him whether he thought that Paul had led the Athenians in prayer before he addressed them on Mars Hill.

Incidentally I have known how embarrassing prayer in an evangelistic meeting can be. I am thinking of a reserved southern Englishman who plucked up courage and invited his highly respectable next-door neighbour to accompany him to an evangelistic meeting. Much to his surprise he agreed to come. Imagine how he felt with his guest sitting beside him when a well-intentioned man led the meeting in prayer 'for the unsaved who have been brought in tonight'! This red-faced Christian told me he felt like crawling under his chair!

I have heard non-Christians suggest that the hymn singing was for the purpose of softening up the audience. Others have confessed to being bored by the whole proceeding. I discovered this as long ago as the early 1950s at the beginning of my ministry, when I used to preach in the open-air at a holiday resort on the south coast of England. It was then possible to draw a large crowd by this means. (I often suspected that people on holiday, away from their home district and friends and neighbours, did not mind being seen standing at a religious meeting where nobody knew them!) It was noticeable, however, that whenever a hymn was announced, the passers-by at the back of the crowd would invariably move on. A prayer had the same effect, and Paul no doubt would have found the same in Athens.

It is surprising, though, how many have assumed that these are essential ingredients of the work of evangelism. I once encountered this when conducting evangelistic missions in American universities. They took place in secular buildings and advertised as lectures. As I was simply setting forth the 'evangel', seeking to persuade my hearers of its truth and urging them to commit themselves to Jesus Christ I thought that what I was doing could be fairly described as evangelism. Yet here is the comment of a University paper. The editorial began, 'Although the Reverend Kenneth F. W. Prior calls his preaching evangelism ...' and then concluded:

> You won't find a 300 voice choir or mass conversions at his lectures this week, but you will encounter an evangelism which is forthright and intellectually honest, rare attractions in the circus world of American evangelism.

I would certainly not want to identify myself with the sweeping innuendo about the 'circus world of American evangelism' of which I have had no experience. Also it was many years ago. But I would ask whether there are still those who wander in their understanding from the simple essentials of true evangelism in the New Testament.

If Paul was to meet people on their own ground, the market place was an obvious choice. Not only would a fair crowd of people be found there, but also it was where religious and philosophical matters were often discussed. And this seems to be forced upon us nowadays as it has become increasingly difficult to persuade people, especially those with no church background, to come out to meetings, whether in a church, hall or tent. It has been by no means a rare experience to speak at an 'evangelistic meeting', and preach one's heart out, and to discover afterwards that there wasn't a single non-Christian present. It is like fishing in a swimming pool!

There may, of course, still be many in Western society without any true Christian commitment, whether or not they could even be described as nominal Christians, who would have no objection to participating in an act of worship. They will be happy, for example, to attend carol services at Christmas. But there is no doubt that they are becoming fewer. I can remember a time when acts of Christian worship in schools were taken for granted and every school would have non-Christian teachers willing to take their turn to conduct it. The situation in Britain today, however, is quite different and there are some schools where it is difficult to find any teacher willing to lead in worship in which he or she does not personally believe.

Ours is not the first generation to have this difficulty. George Whitefield discovered in the eighteenth
century that most of those he longed to reach with
the gospel would never enter a church to hear it. So
the only way was to go out into the open air and
preach there. Many, including John Wesley, had to
be persuaded that it was permissible to preach any-
where other than in church. Open air meetings of
that kind may not necessarily be the modern equivalent of the market place which will vary in different
parts of the world. John Stott suggests

> a park, city square or street corner, a shopping mall or
> market place, a 'pub', neighbourhood bar, cafe, dis-
> cotheque or student cafeteria, wherever people meet
> when they are at leisure. [1]

It could be that people are best reached in their own
or our homes over a meal. Whatever the actual
method, the principle we learn from Paul, not only
from his time in Athens but from his entire missionary career, is that people are reached not by expecting them to come to us, but by us going to them.

If what we have just described is the way to reach
complete pagans, then this changes the whole style
of evangelism and the gifts demanded of the evangelist. We have come to regard him as someone with
the gift of preaching to the unconverted, who visits a
district for this purpose with or without the invitation of local churches. It is the latter who have the
task of preparing for his mission by visiting non-
Christians and inviting them to come and hear the

gospel. This is no easy task as is usually discovered, yet the visiting evangelist depends on it if he is to have an audience.

Recently someone was describing to me a mission held at their church which consisted largely of meetings night by night addressed by the visiting evangelist. They did, however, have one or two extra meetings specially designed to reach complete outsiders. Much effort went into preparation by way of visiting and attempts at establishing relationships with those they were trying to reach. But, to their great disappointment, no one came. To add to their discomfiture, the evangelist failed to conceal his annoyance at their failure. Yet I have to admit that for me, at least, it is far easier to preach an evangelistic sermon than to draw together a congregation of unbelievers with no Christian background to listen to me.

It goes without saying that when Paul arrived in Athens there was no church there to prepare for his coming. If unbelievers were to hear the gospel from his lips he had to make contact with them himself. It was in the ability to do this that the gift of an evangelist (e.g. Ephesians 4:11) in New Testament times largely lay. Contrary to this, I have heard at conferences on evangelism the gift of an evangelist being assumed to be the ability to 'make an appeal' and 'draw in the net' at the end of a meeting.

If the gift of evangelism consists largely in breaking new ground and directly confronting non-Christians with the gospel where they are, we must recognise that it is not a gift shared by every Christian, nor is it meant to be. At this point I would like the reader to turn to Colossians 4:3-6. In verses 3-4 Paul asks his readers to pray for his work as an evangelist. Then in verses 5-6 he tells his readers what he expects them to contribute to the task of spreading the gospel. This includes the way they live and what they say. But there is a significant difference between the obligation under which Paul finds himself from that which he places upon his readers. R. C. Lucas has drawn what seems to be the right conclusion and I quote him in full:

> A comparison between the two final phrases in each half of the section shows a difference in emphasis of some significance. They are to pray for the apostle that he might make the gospel known *as he ought to speak*. He in turn gives them sound advice so that they may know how they *ought to answer* everyone.
>
> We may describe this difference by saying that while the apostle looks for many opportunities for *direct* evangelism and teaching, the typical Christian in Colossae is to look for many opportunities for *responsive* evangelism.
>
> If this distinction is a correct one, it immediately commends itself by its sanity and realism. Harm can be done by sincere believing people who feel compelled to preach and testify to those with whom they mix in shop or office. Rightly aware of the importance of their message, the sad ignorance of many of their neighbours, and the urgency of the times, they plunge in bravely (whatever the temperature!). But direct assault on entrenched apathy (to change the metaphor)

is seldom successful and can never be carried out by normally sensitive people without great cost to nerve and confidence ....Their privilege, simply put, is to *answer everyone*. That is to say they are to respond to the questions of others rather than initiate conversations on leading topics; they are to *accept* openings rather than *make* them.[2]

The implication is that if you are 'wise in the way you act towards outsiders' and 'make the most of every opportunity' you will not lack openings to speak. Peter had the same expectations of his readers (1 Peter 3:15).

In Athens Paul was clearly engaged in what R. C. Lucas calls 'direct evangelism'. And if we are to follow Paul's example today we clearly need church members with this gift. In a local church, alongside the pastor-teacher we need the evangelist(s) in the sense we are now using that word. Whether it is a full-time post or unpaid will depend on local circumstances. Perhaps when we are seeking 'gifts' for a church fellowship this ought to come high on our list of priorities. We also need those who will operate on a wider scale beyond the local church. As John Stott sees it,

> there is an urgent need for more Christian thinkers who will dedicate their minds to Christ, not only as lecturers, but also as authors, journalists, dramatists and broadcasters, as television script-writers, producers and personalities, and as artists and actors who use a variety of art forms in which to communicate the gospel.[3]

At any rate, there is obviously a need for much discussion if we are to apply this principle of Paul's ministry to the evangelistic task of today.

Once Paul was out among the people of Athens, how did he present the claims of Christ? Luke uses just one word: he 'reasoned' (verse 34). This and other similar words such as 'argue', 'prove', 'dispute', 'debate' repeatedly occur in our English translations of Acts, to describe the way that Paul presented his case both to the Jews in the synagogues and to the Greeks (9:22,29; 17:2,3; 18:4,19,28; 19:8,9; 24:25). Expressions such as these can leave us in no doubt about Paul's normal aim which was to convince people's minds of the truth of the gospel as the means of persuading them to submit their wills.

This emphasis on the mind is found throughout Scripture. Everywhere the appeal is to the understanding, whether it is Old Testament historian, poet or prophet, or New Testament apostle. Also it applies to the entire Christian life. To begin with, apostate Israel was called upon to entertain the gospel of forgiveness with the appeal, '"Come, now, let us reason together," says the LORD ...' (Isaiah 1:18). Prophets, apostles and Jesus himself call upon people to come to God in repentance, and this means literally a change of mind. A person who has come to God in this way will then make progress in the Christian life 'by the renewing of your mind' (Rom. 12:1). Paul also sees the warfare in which a Christian is engaged as essentially a battle for the mind:

> The weapons we fight with are not the weapons of the world. On the contrary they have divine power to demolish strongholds. We demolish arguments and every pretension that sets itself up against the knowledge of God, and we take captive every thought to make it obedient to Christ (2 Corinthians 10:4-5).

And when it comes to witness before unbelievers ('responsive evangelism', as we have called it), it is to 'be prepared to give an answer to everyone who asks you to give the *reason* for the hope that you have' (1 Peter 3:15).

Not every modern evangelist has made quite the same effort to convince people's minds of the truth of Christianity. Indeed I remember reading some years ago in a book by a fairly prominent evangelist, the remarkable statement that emotion is the driving force of the gospel! Not surprisingly he produced no Scriptural backing for this assertion, which was presumably based on experience of his own methods. Sometimes there has been a conscious reluctance to appeal to the mind out of an awareness that mere head knowledge won't save a person. We heartily agree. The will must be submitted to the claims of Christ. But no one can do this without knowledge of the gospel, and how, in view of the way that God has created us, do we know anything except with our heads? 'No one was ever argued into the Kingdom of God', it has sometimes been said. Again, we agree, if this means that human argument alone is insufficient. But that does not free us from the obligation to use reasoned argument. Man has been created with a mind and God expects him to use it in understanding the truth he has made known.

We must, however, recognise that, important though the use of the mind is, human argument alone is insufficient to bring unbelievers to a knowledge of God's truth. It is a solemn fact that sin has distorted unbelieving minds. As a result, apart from the intervention of the Holy Spirit, they are not just waiting for the first Christian to explain the gospel and tell them why it is true, before they capitulate to its claims. Paul knew only too well what lay at the root of their difficulties: 'The god of this age has blinded the minds of unbelievers, so that they cannot see the light of the gospel of the glory of Christ...' (2 Corinthians 4:4).

I remember how this was brought home to me when I was addressing a group of University lecturers. One might have assumed that if unaided intellect was sufficient for discovering the truth of the gospel-trained minds such as theirs would have no difficulty. Such was not my experience of that highly intellectual group. In the discussion which followed my talk a professor of physics employed the most fatuous arguments to undermine what I had said. I asked him if he would have employed the same kind of 'reasoning' in physics. He was at least honest enough to admit that he would not. It was apparent that there were factors other than pure reason operating when he was confronted with the claims of Christ.

Such a condition demands more than a human

remedy and so the ultimate cause why some have seen the truth of the gospel is that 'God who said, "Let light shine out of darkness," made his light shine in our hearts to give us the light of the knowledge of the glory of God in the face of Christ' (2 Corinthians 4:6).

How does God bring this about? By ignoring our fallen minds and appealing instead to our feelings and emotions? There is little future in that course since they are just as fallen as our minds. God's way is not to bypass the understanding but to stimulate and enlighten it. But this calls for a miracle which, in the above quotation, Paul puts on a level with the way in which, at the command of God, light first penetrated the primeval darkness at the creation. But miracle though it is, it is still the mind that has to be enlightened.

Paul's Ephesian readers provide an example of this. He first reminds them of how unconverted Gentiles live 'in the futility of their thinking. They are darkened in their understanding and separated from the life of God because of the ignorance that is in them due to the hardening of their hearts' (Ephesians 4:17-18).

What had happened to his readers that had rendered them so different from other Gentiles? Something had happened to their minds. Here is how Paul describes it:

You, however, did not come to know Christ in that way. Surely you have heard of him and were *taught* in accordance with the truth that is in Jesus. You were *taught*,

with regard to your former way of life ... to be made
new in the attitude of your *minds* (Ephesians 4:20-23).

God, then, does not ignore people's minds and neither should we. Here is how J. I. Packer summarised
it:

> The duty of Christian witness involves reasoning, as
> the descriptions of Paul's missionary activity show.
> Faith is not created by reasoning, but neither is it cre-
> ated without it. There is more involved in witness to
> Christ than throwing pre-arranged clumps of texts at
> unbelieving heads; the meaning and application of the
> gospel must be explained to men and women in terms
> of their actual situation. This requires hard thinking. [4]

As we shall see later, the explaining of the gospel 'to
men and women in terms of their actual situation'
was precisely what Paul did in Athens.

Now it must be admitted that this emphasis on
the mind is not the way many questions are settled in
the last part of the twentieth century. Whether we
like it or not, reasoned argument is not the usual way
in which the masses of people are influenced today.

Take for example advertising which is constantly
being aimed at all of us. The way in which it seeks to
condition our choices lacks any appeal to reason. The
television commercial, to take one of the most influ-
ential vehicles of advertising, rarely if ever employs
rational argument for preferring one brand of a product to all others. Instead, the advertiser plays on the
fears and insecurities of the viewing public and
attempts to create the longings which a particular

product is supposed to satisfy. The young woman advertising a particular brand of toothpaste with a smile which reveals her sparkling teeth is surrounded by male admirers. Whether it destroys the bacteria which cause tooth decay is quite beside the point! Then a virile looking young man appears on the screen, just the kind of person an inadequate young male viewer dreams of being. And what is the secret? Of course it is the brand of beer he is drinking as he leans nonchalantly against the bar counter. Politics seems increasingly to follow the same tack with advertising firms employed to improve the image of a candidate or party aspiring to political power.

How is the evangelist going to set about convincing people that the gospel he offers is true, will work and is just what they need? Is he to assault them with the techniques we have described? If he is the conductor of large rallies he has some opportunity to do so. He can advertise himself so as to build up his image. If he can draw a crowd there are ways in which he can manipulate them. Adolf Hitler was a genius at this and discovered what he could do with a stadium full of young people by getting them to chant repeatedly, 'Ein Volk, ein Reich, ein Führer'. An evangelist can use repetitive and rhythmical singing with the same effect. Sentimentality in the choice of music can produce 'results'. A story graphically told can be more than just an illustration, but can be used to heighten tension in a meeting. We feel entitled to ask whether any real conversions are produced by such methods.

Needless to say these and other ways of bypassing the intellect have no place in Scripture. The appeal is always first to the mind with a view to the will being challenged to respond. Emotions such as fear, love, joy and wonder might well be aroused, but it was the result of being convinced about the truth and not vice-versa. This did not necessarily involve long and intricate reasoning. In the market place Paul may well have given them small doses and been content to take his hearers a short distance at a time, as he did with the uneducated farming community at Lystra in Acts 14. Nor do we have to indulge in abstract philosophical notions. Most people think in concrete terms. Our Lord made copious use of illustrations, mostly from nature and agriculture, when speaking to the crowds. We know from Paul's writings that he too could use analogy. And, as we shall see, he spoke in concrete terms in Athens.

These provisos, however, do not mean that we avoid the intellect altogether when presenting Christian truth. Rather it is part of our task to expose the irrationality of today's world. If God has created us with minds, he intends us to use them. And this is the way by which he expects us to find him and be led by him, as he expressed it through the psalmist:

> I will instruct you and teach you in the way you should go; I will counsel you and watch over you. Do not be like the horse or the mule, which have no understanding (Psalm 32:8-9).

If we are to argue our case effectively, not only

do we need to be masters of what we believe and why, but we must also appreciate the outlook and problems of those we are trying to reach. Otherwise we are in very real danger of talking at cross purposes. Failure to observe this principle of communication may well lie at the heart of some of our difficulties in evangelism today. But Paul did not fall into this mistake, as will begin to become apparent in our next chapter.

4

CHANCE OR FATE?

We must now consider the implications of a very significant detail which Luke gives us: 'A group of Epicurean and Stoic philosophers began to dispute with him' (Acts 17:18). Now why should Luke bother to include this piece of information?

During recent years the thinking of many Christians has been influenced by Francis Schaeffer and the L'Abri Fellowship. Whether or not one goes all the way with his views, one cannot resist the good sense of his general approach. Here is how he described it as he began his first book:

> If a man goes overseas for any length of time we would expect him to learn the language of the country to which he is going. More than this is needed, however, if he is really to communicate with the people among whom he is living. He must learn another language – that of the thought forms of the people to whom he speaks. Only then will he have real communication with them and to them. So it is with the Christian Church. Its responsibility is not only to hold to the basic, scriptural principles of the Christian faith, but to communicate these unchanging truths 'into' the generation in which it is living. [1]

Schaeffer's book is then devoted to the philosophical ideas and their history which lie behind the outlook and thinking of people today.

Now the Epicurean and Stoic philosophies had that kind of influence in Greek and Roman society of Paul's day. When we come to the Areopagus address itself we shall discover that Paul had taken the trouble to understand the thinking of his hearers and so spoke relevantly to them. Especially is there every indication that he appreciated the shortcomings of both systems of philosophy.

Our Lord in his ministry to individuals showed the same awareness of the needs of the people he was seeking to help. The classical example is the way he dealt with the Samaritan woman in John 4. His approach to her was shaped not only by the truth he wished to convey, but also by the problems arising both from her background as a Samaritan, and from the particular sins of which she was guilty. This meant that he had no cut and dried method for all and sundry, but rather his approach varied from one individual to another. This also applied to his healing ministry, which affords some striking examples. One is the man who suffered from deafness and an impediment in his speech (Mark 7:31-37). Those who brought him to Jesus assumed that he would simply 'place his hand upon the man', as they had seen him do with others. But Jesus was not tied to any fixed method. Instead he perceived that in order to awaken faith in a man who suffered from deafness as well as a speech defect, a different form of treatment was called for. Jesus' method of communication with him was restricted to sign language except for the Aramaic for 'be opened', 'ephphatha' which would be easy to lip read.

In the light of this we ought to examine those methods of evangelism which prescribe a set of points to be almost mechanically applied to the potential convert. No provision is made for listening to what the unbeliever has to say, with a view to understanding his problems and discovering the point at which the gospel applies to his need. When I was a young minister I spoke to a senior colleague about an unbeliever I had tried unsuccessfully to help. 'What is the greatest difficulty standing in the way of him becoming a Christian?' he asked. I had no idea. In my enthusiasm to apply familiar texts, I had never bothered to find out.

Now admittedly if a Christian perseveres with a stereotyped approach he is likely to meet with some success, as sooner or later he will presumably encounter someone to whom the way he presents the gospel applies. Furthermore, knowing what we do about the sovereign grace of God, we shall not be surprised if sooner or later the believer is rewarded with a contact which fits his approach. Also, we have no doubt, that learning these methods is often a great help to a Christian in impressing on his or her own mind the basic points of the gospel. What our present study demands is that we should add to these basic essentials a greater awareness of the outlook of those we are trying to reach, and, as a consequence, apply them in a more flexible and imaginative manner.

Herein lies the strength of evangelistic writers like Michael Green. One of his earlier evangelistic books was *Man Alive* on the evidences for the resurrection. Not only does he marshal his arguments with characteristic skill, but applies them to the futility of the outlook of many today which he describes in his opening chapter under the heading, 'More dead than alive'. He demonstrates that the spiritual death that pervades today's society is a 'modern predicament' that is not essentially different from the 'ancient predicament', to use his sub-headings. Into this context he introduces his theme which, as we shall see, is virtually that of Paul in Athens, 'Jesus and the resurrection'. [2]

Some may wonder what the Epicurean and Stoic philosophies had to do with many of the people Paul encountered in the market place. Unlike the intelligentsia he addressed on Mars Hill, not all of those he spoke to would have been versed in philosophy, and the way in which he was misunderstood by a section of his hearers, who thought he was offering them two extra deities, suggests that some of them at least were not outstandingly bright! The same could be asked about taking into account the speculations of modern thinkers, when contemplating the evangelisation of the semi-educated masses today.

We sometimes fail to appreciate the influence of philosophical systems. The two to which Luke draws our attention may at first sight seem far removed from the popular religion of Athens which was represented by the crude forms of idolatry which affected Paul. Yet their influence was by no means confined to the frequenters of libraries. Indeed, as we shall see, these two philosophies also reflect the outlook of masses of ordinary people at the end of the twentieth century. The same can be said of recent examples. Names like Kirkegaard of the nineteenth century and twentieth-century writers such as Sartre and Camus have probably never been heard of by most people, but their existentialism represents a way of thinking that is found everywhere.

So we now turn to a brief description of the Epicurean and Stoic philosophies. The former is named after Epicurus, whose dates were 341-270 BC. He is best known for his views of ethics, that 'good' is what brings most pleasure. The utilitarianism of John Stuart Mills is a nineteenth-century refinement of this position, where the aim becomes 'the greatest happiness of the greatest number'. That just about sums up the only basis for living that many today have found. You are free to do just what you like ('your own thing') provided that it does not interfere with the happiness of anyone else.

Lying behind this was the theological view of Epicurus. He was not strictly speaking an atheist, although to all intents and purposes he might well have been, because he taught that the gods, whatever they may have done in creating the world, have no further interest in it. All that happens now is simply the result of chance. There is no life beyond the grave as death ends everything. There is ultimately nothing to fear and nothing to hope for. As far as this life is concerned their motto could well be, as Paul would have put it, 'eat, drink and be merry, for tomorrow we die', although to be fair to Epicurus and his immediate followers, they did not pursue their views to this, their logical conclusion.

It is not difficult to see that the stress on chance underlies the outlook of multitudes of people in the twentieth century, although few of them will have heard of Epicurus. Everything is the result of 'luck'. When things go wrong you are 'down on your luck'. Casinos, bingo halls, betting shops and football pools are patronized by vast numbers with the distant hope of a 'lucky break' which will change their fortune overnight. The present addiction to gambling shows how widespread this outlook is. The Mintel survey in 1992 revealed that in Britain four out of ten people questioned admitted to placing some sort of bet at least once a fortnight which added up to £12.2 billion being staked over the previous year. During the first three months of the National Lottery introduced in the autumn of 1994, average weekly ticket sales amounted to more than £56 million. Neil Collins, City Editor of *The Daily Telegraph,* described the National Lottery in November, 1994 as 'the most elegant way yet devised of taking money from the poor and redistributing it to the rich.' 'The British are a nation of gambling addicts' commented the *Daily Mail* in July, 1992. The situation is no better in the United States. According to *Christianity Today* (November, 1991) Americans were then placing legal bets worth over $286 billion a year. Whether the motive is the hope of making money or simply for fun, it means that vast numbers of people spend time and energy appealing to chance. I well remember someone defending her 'weekly flutter' by saying that all life is a gamble and every time you cross a busy street you risk your life. The god who ruled her life was certainly chance.

Then there were the Stoics. Their ideas were first propounded by Zeno (335-263 BC), although there were others who produced their own modifications. What their position amounted to was that the affairs of this world are directed by a blind, impersonal but rational force within it, sometimes called a 'world-soul'. This view is also quite common in the twentieth century, only instead of 'world-soul' other terms will be used such as 'Nature' spelling it with a capital 'N', as the force at work in creation. Sometimes it will be almost personalised by calling it 'Mother Nature'. Theologians would describe this view as 'pantheistic'. Although it can take on a variety of forms, it basically holds that God is wholly immanent in the world. Whether he is identified with creation, or contained within it, there is nothing of God outside of it.

Like every theory of life, Stoicism has a way of living based upon it. The blind force within creation is often called 'fate' and the most satisfactory way of living is not to engage in a pointless struggle against it but to ally yourself with it. Accept things as they are, no matter how painful, and in so doing you will be on the side of the inherent reason, as they often called it, within the universe. You must not allow your emotions to take control, but you must ensure your attitude is always subject to reason. This is the way of contentment and peace of mind.

Here was an outlook which made a strong appeal to the Roman mind, and it numbered some prominent names among its adherents, such as the emperor, Marcus Aurelius. It is patently the complete opposite of the Epicurean approach to life. Instead of being tossed about by chance, the happenings of this world are determined by fate, and a cold, impersonal and merciless thing it is. It comes naturally to many to embrace fatalism when life is difficult. Accepting things as they are without emotion is often called keeping a 'stiff upper lip'. It flourishes in wartime when you resign yourself to the view that if the bullet or the bomb has 'got your name on it' it will get you whatever you do. It is quite surprising how those whose lifestyle is based on chance can quite easily swing to the other extreme and resign themselves to fate when faced with a question that seems to be conveniently answered that way. A few years ago I saw on television a succession of passers-by being asked if they intended to give up smoking in view of the hazard to health it entails. A surprising number said they would not and advanced the reason that, if fate has determined that you are going to die soon you will die whatever precautions you take. If it is not through lung cancer, you will probably be run over in the street, so why worry? One cannot deny that such an attitude has its uses if you can sustain it!

Now the observation which has an important bearing on our theme, is that these two systems represent the only two alternatives to the personal God of biblical revelation. If you don't believe that in the last analysis the affairs of this world are ordered by a personal God who is quite distinct from his creatures and yet has a personal relationship with them, what else is there? One alternative is that the universe, the earth, life, human personality and all that befalls us are one gigantic fluke. The only other alternative is that there is some impersonal force at work. As far as our lives are concerned, either they are at the mercy of a frivolous thing called chance, or in the pitiless grip of a cold impersonal fate. [3]

These issues tend to come to the fore when the problem of suffering is under discussion. A Christian often finds it hard to explain it in terms of a personal God. But what are the alternatives? Whether suffering arises from chance or fate, either way there is no hope, and that is far worse than the seemingly unsatisfactory explanations to which Christians often resort.

The comment of Professor F. F. Bruce aptly summarises the position:

Stoicism and Epicureanism represent alternative attempts in pre-Christian paganism to come to terms with life, especially in times of uncertainty and hardship, and post-Christian paganism has not been able to devise anything appreciably better. [4]

5

JESUS AND THE RESURRECTION

Having drawn our attention to the two schools of
thought represented among Paul's hearers, Luke proceeds to describe the way in which Paul's efforts in
the market place were received. We shall pay attention to that in our next chapter, but first we must
amplify what we said in Chapter 3 about Paul's use
of reasoned argument. It was very different from the
way the thinkers of Ancient Greece used their minds
in the quest for truth, the limitations of which we
shall examine more closely in Chapter 7. Paul did
not make Greek ideas his starting point and try to
show how the gospel fitted them, nor did he reason
in a vacuum as many of his hearers would have done.
Rather he reasoned around two basic facts: the Jesus
of history and his resurrection. This is readily inferred from the way his hearers reacted to him:

> Some of them asked, 'What is this babbler trying to
> say?' Others remarked, 'He seems to be advocating
> foreign gods.' They said this because Paul was preach-
> ing the good news about Jesus and the resurrection
> (Acts 17:18).

There may well have been other gospel truths to
which he referred, but according to the impression

gained by many in his audience, these were the two basic facts that lay at the heart of his argument for the truth of Christianity – 'Jesus and the resurrection'.

The person of Christ lay at the centre of all the apostolic preaching recorded in the Acts, not least that of Paul himself. Immediately after his conversion we find him in Damascus, 'proving that Jesus is the Christ' (Acts 9:22). Right through his ministry he maintained the same emphasis. Only just before his visit to Athens he had spent three successive Sabbaths in the synagogue at Thessalonica and 'reasoned with them from the Scriptures, explaining and proving that the Christ had to suffer and rise from the dead. "This Jesus I am proclaiming to you is the Christ," ' he said (Acts 17:2-3). At the end of Acts his theme has not changed as he 'tried to convince them about Jesus from the Law of Moses and from the Prophets' (Acts 28:23).

In Athens, so it seems, he pursued the same course. Once he had left the synagogue and was among the Gentiles in the market place, we would not expect him to prove that Jesus was the Christ of Old Testament prophecy. In the early chapters of his letter to the Romans it is most noticeable that when addressing Gentiles from 1:18 to 2:16 he makes no Old Testament quotations, although he does so from 2:17 onwards when he is addressing the Jews. In the Areopagus address, it is true, there are marks of Old Testament teaching, but there are no direct quotations, nor does Paul appeal to its authority to enforce what he is saying. But Luke, in this example of how Paul approached complete pagans, wants us to know that although he did not identify Jesus with the Christ of Old Testament anticipation, he still centred his case for Christianity on the person of Jesus.

Paul would have seen Gentiles being reached in this way at Antioch when he first made it his home church. To begin with the New Testament church had been remarkably reluctant over direct evangelism of the Gentiles. Peter found that baptizing Cornelius took some explaining, but when they heard what had happened, members of the Jerusalem church dropped their objections and praised God that he had 'granted even the Gentiles repentance unto life' (Acts 11:18). But even then those scattered from Jerusalem by the persecution following Stephen's martyrdom told 'the message only to Jews' (Acts 11:19). At Antioch, however came a turning point when some began to speak to Gentiles. As a result 'a great number of people believed and turned to the Lord' (Acts 11:21).

Barnabas was sent to Antioch by the Jerusalem church to investigate and he was greatly encouraged by what he saw. He must have known that Paul was called to be the apostle to the Gentiles, because his immediate reaction was to go to Tarsus and persuade him to move to Antioch, presumably to experience for himself what was going on there. He and Barnabas immediately threw themselves wholeheartedly into the work, while Paul made Antioch his home church where he spent his leave between his missionary journeys. But notice Luke's simple statement of how this Gentile evangelism at Antioch began:

> Men from Cyprus and Cyrene went to Antioch and began to speak to Greeks also, telling them *the good news about the Lord Jesus* (Acts 11:20).

This has always been the hallmark of true evangelism. How often John Wesley recorded in his diary: 'I came into the town and offered them Christ'. It is the reason why John's Gospel has so often been used to good effect in evangelism, especially among those who have been avowed unbelievers, for this is its declared purpose. The writer himself explains that this aim governed his choice of material from the many miracles and discourses at his disposal from the life of Christ:

> Jesus did many other miraculous signs in the presence of his disciples, which are not recorded in this book. But these are written that you may believe that Jesus is the Christ, the Son of God, and that by believing you may have life in his name (John 20:30-31).

At this stage a caution ought to be sounded because of the way that 'Jesus' has become a popular figure in recent times, even to the extent of being a character suitable for the stage. We need constantly to ask whether the 'Jesus' being presented is really the Jesus whom Paul and the other apostles presented, remembering Paul's own warning about anyone who 'comes to you and preaches a Jesus other than the Jesus we preached' (2 Corinthians 11:4). To the Colossians, who were being presented with a Jesus who

fitted the notions of Greek philosophy, he gave a reminder that the Jesus he preached was one in whom
'all the fulness of the Deity lives in bodily form'
(Colossians 2:9).

Some writers blatantly use Jesus as a character in
their novels with no regard for history, even to the
extent of attributing low moral standards to him.
More subtle was Dennis Potter's *Son of Man* which I
remember watching on television some years ago. I
could not imagine anyone saying to his version of
Jesus 'You have the words of eternal life' (John 6:68).
Still less would anyone have acclaimed him 'the
Christ, the Son of the living God' (Matthew 16:16).
It was difficult to resist the conclusion that the whole
play was a deliberate humanist attempt to reduce
Jesus to the size that suits the presuppositions of those
who deny the supernatural.

Now the Jesus presented by the apostles in their
writings will not fit the limits of such thinking. He
made uncompromising claims about himself, such
as the power to forgive sins and to give eternal life.
He declared that one day he will appear again as the
judge of the whole world. With God he claimed a
unique relationship, so that those who had seen him
had seen God the Father, and he like God was to be
the object of religious faith. This was also the Jesus
whom Paul preached, and that this was the main di-
rection of his argument may be inferred from the
impression of some of his hearers that he was setting up Jesus as another deity.

The other emphasis in Paul's argument which

made an impact upon his hearers was the resurrection. This too was constantly on apostolic lips as they testified to the truth of the gospel. The reason why they were so sure that it was a fact of history was simply that they were witnesses of the event, as they repeatedly claimed.[1] Paul makes it quite clear that he too was well aware of this apostolic witness to the resurrection (Acts 13:30-31). Indeed he gives a detailed account of it to the church at Corinth, and actually numbers himself among the witnesses, regarding his conversion experience on the Damascus Road in this way (1 Corinthians 15:1-9). And being a witness of the resurrection was what entitled him to call himself an apostle (1 Corinthians 9:1). To the early Christians the resurrection was the supreme evidence for the truth of Christianity. It was the sign to which Jesus had pointed when he refused to give other signs (Matthew 12:38-40).

Now it seems not unreasonable to conclude that this was how Paul was using the resurrection in Athens when he linked it with the person of Jesus. He made the same connection when writing to the Romans pointing out that Jesus 'was declared with power to be the Son of God by his resurrection from the dead: Jesus Christ our Lord' (Romans 1:4).

That Paul was using the fact of the resurrection to confirm the truth of Christianity is further indicated by the way he returns to it right at the end of the Areopagus address. Here Paul underlines the certainty of what he has been saying by affirming of it that God 'has given proof of this to all men by raising him from the dead' (Acts 17:31). This then was his own explanation of why he had been arguing about 'Jesus and the resurrection' in the market place.

An obvious question to ask is how we follow the apostles' example in using the fact of the resurrection to establish the truth of what we believe about Jesus and the gospel. Unlike the first Christians, we have not had the advantage of seeing the risen Christ with our physical eyes. How then can this witness to the resurrection have an impact on unbelieving minds today? The way that some Christians get over this difficulty is to offer a kind of witness very different from that of the apostles, feeling that this is the best they can do. Their answer to an enquirer could be expressed in the words of a well-known couplet:

> You ask me how I know he lives?
> He lives within my heart.

In other words, for the apostles' witness to the resurrection as an objective, historical fact, they substitute a subjective, inward experience, such as feelings of peace or joy.

It is, however, questionable whether we are entitled to apply references to the apostolic witness to every Christian. Michael Green's comment about Luke's use of the word 'witness' merits serious consideration, even if it means revising sermons we have preached on statements like 'you will be my witnesses' (Acts 1:8)!

He has a strong tendency to restrict the word 'witnesses' to those who had known the incarnate Jesus. This is true of all the references apart from the last three in Acts. The witnesses are the people who have lived through the events of Good Friday and Easter, and who can bear personal testimony both to their historicity and to their interpretation. It is because of this function of the witness to guarantee, so to speak, the continuity between the Jesus of history and the Christ of faith, that Paul has to refer in 13:31 not to 'us witnesses' (he was not in this sense), but to 'those who are now witnesses to the people'. [2]

Those who rely on subjective experience as a basis for belief may find themselves in unexpected company because, evangelicals though they would undoubtedly claim to be, their approach is not all that far removed from theologians like Rudolph Bultmann. The difference is that the latter would go further and disclaim all interest in whether the resurrection was an event in history at all. What matters, so they say, is a present experience of the risen Christ, and this does not depend on whether the body of Jesus was left to decay in the tomb or not. Paul clearly thought otherwise, and with all due respects to modern theologians, some of us, at least, still regard him as a more reliable guide to what is essential to the Christian faith. What Paul said in the following, for example, is somewhat different from the idea that it does not matter whether or not Christ rose again provided you enjoy an experience of his risen life:

> If Christ has not been raised, our preaching is useless
> and so is your faith. More than that, we are then found
> to be false witnesses about God, for we have testified
> about God that he raised Christ from the dead. But he
> did not raise him if in fact the dead are not raised ...
> And if Christ has not been raised, your faith is futile;
> you are still in your sins (1 Corinthians 15:14-17).

It is worth noticing that the New Testament Christians never attempted to establish the truth of Christianity by appealing to their inward experiences. Other people may have taken note of a change in their lives, but that is another matter. To be sure they would not have rested content with the resurrection simply as a fact of bare history. Paul claimed that he had experienced the risen life when, for example, he declared, 'Christ lives in me' (Galatians 2:20). That, however, does not mean that he ever advanced this experience as the ground on which others ought to believe. To put it another way, never do we find him trying to prove the truth of Christianity to others 'because of the difference it has made to my life'.

Appealing to our experiences is open to the objection that other faiths and cults do the same. I well remember hearing a young man's testimony to the deep sense of peace and joy he had found. His language reminded me of that used by many a young evangelical. He was referring, however, to what he had found through a mystical Eastern religion. There was no reason to doubt the validity of the experience he claimed, but that did not establish the truth of the doctrines on which it was based.

What is the lesson in all this for Christians today? It is surely that our primary task is not to press upon others our own experience, important though this may be to ourselves, but rather to expose them to the testimony of the apostles to the resurrection as an historical event. It may be asked how we can do that 2,000 years after the apostles lived. The answer is quite simple – we have the claims they made for Jesus, both his person and resurrection, in the writings they have left us. The unbeliever may be unwilling to share the Christian belief that they are inspired and constitute the 'Word of God', but the writings of the first Christians have the right to be taken seriously. After all, no one thinks that historians of ancient Rome such as Livy and Tacitus were inspired by God, but that does not prevent us from giving due considerations to the records they have left to us. So the claims the first Christians made about Jesus, which they set out in their writings, demand a verdict.

Bultmann, in the course of his so-called demythologising, makes the assertion: 'All that historical criticism can establish is the fact that the first disciples came to believe in the resurrection.'[3] But this is also an admission. It is that we can be sure that the disciples did, in fact, claim that Jesus rose from the dead. The challenge to the unbelieving mind, whether in the Athens of the first century or in sophisticated circles of the twentieth, is to determine the origin of that belief. Was it based on fact, was it a clever hoax, or just a colossal mistake?

The suggestion that it was all a deliberate fabrication does seem a bit far-fetched. A group of uneducated fishermen are supposed to have pulled off the hoax only six weeks after the event and within fifteen minutes walk of the tomb, and convinced a large number of people. Why couldn't the Jewish leaders put a stop to the new movement by taking people on a visit to the tomb, unless the disciples stole the body? But would they have done such a thing and then be prepared to be martyred for what they knew to be untrue? As Pascal once said, 'I readily believe those witnesses who are willing to have their throats cut.'

Perhaps it was all a mistake and the disciples were suffering from an illusion. But such a mistake could easily be rectified by producing the body.

So was the resurrection a fact? Paul saw no reason for shielding the secular minds of his day from the choice, so why should we today? Don't tell me that the all-important difference between then and now is that ours is a scientific age. Is this meant to imply that it was easier to accept a bodily resurrection in a pre-scientific age than now? There is no evidence that it was. Paul knew that the claim he was making would stretch their credulity as it did when he referred to it in his address to the Areopagus council and 'some of them sneered' (Acts 17:32). That he persisted in his claims for the resurrection only goes to show that he was certain of his facts. It is no different today. The rise of modern physics has not made it more or less easy to accept a supernatural event like the resurrection.

We have to face, of course, that in a secular society there are many who find it difficult to believe in anything supernatural. When confronted with a miraculous event like the resurrection, their built-in reaction is to try to explain it away, and the lengths to which some will go in doing so are truly remarkable. An extreme example is what has usually been called the Swoon theory.

The suggestion is that Jesus did not die on the cross but only fainted. It so happened that the authorities forgot to ensure that Jesus was dead, as they usually did with victims of judicial crucifixion. As a consequence he was interred unconscious but still alive. Then after three days something very unexpected is supposed to have happened. Despite his desperate physical condition and lack of medical attention, he revived. Still more remarkably, he extricated himself from the grave clothes in which, in accordance with custom, he would have been bound from his neck down to his feet. Then, severely wounded and weak though he was, he succeeded in rolling the heavy stone to one side, a feat difficult enough for someone in the best of health. How he managed to move the stone with his wounded hands with nothing to grip on its flat surface has not been explained. Next he sought out his disciples, who had fled in terror at his crucifixion, and convinced them that he had risen from the dead! Jesus then conveniently disappeared from the scene. This has been advanced as a serious explanation. It surely demonstrates how desperate some have been to avoid anything supernatural, preferring a ridiculous natural explanation to a perfectly sensible supernatural one.

And what we have just described is by no means the only evasion which has been tried. Another is the suggestion that the New Testament narratives were no more than an attempt on the part of the early church to express their conviction about the triumph and exaltation of Jesus. And this is in spite of the early date of 1 Corinthians in which Paul refers to witnesses of the resurrection who were still alive when he was writing. Paul must have been aware of this kind of prejudice in his own day, when he addressed King Agrippa, 'Why should any of you think it incredible that God raises the dead?' (Acts 26:8)

With those who argue that a resurrection would be a highly unusual event, the answer is to agree. Jesus was an unusual person. If in his person God himself was intervening in the world's history, and making a special revelation of himself, would it not be more surprising if miracles did not occur? Of course they do not take place in the normal course of history, but the life, death and resurrection of Jesus were not part of the 'normal course of history'. Indeed, we can go further with Lesslie Newbigin:

> It is obvious that the story of the empty tomb cannot be fitted into our contemporary worldview, or into any worldview of which it is the starting point ....What happened on that day is, according to the Christian tradition, only to be understood by analogy with what happened on the day the cosmos came into being. It is

a boundary event, at the point where (as cosmologists tell us) the laws of physics cease to apply. It is the beginning of a new creation – as mysterious to human reason as the creation itself. [4]

So the only honest approach is to examine the evidence for the resurrection with an open mind, without begging the question with the presupposition that because it was a miracle it could not have happened.

To go into all the evidence is beyond our present scope. It is however well worth noting that many who have studied it have found it overwhelming. Of the many books which have been written setting it out there is one by Frank Morison who intended in the first place to write a book disproving the resurrection. He describes it, however, in the title of his first chapter as 'The book that refused to be written' for the evidence drove him to the opposite conclusion. [5]

It may well be asked what unbelievers, who persist in their unbelief, have to say about the resurrection. That is not an easy question to answer. To pretend that they all hold to fantastic explanations like the Swoon theory would hardly do many of them justice. What many apparently do is to ignore it altogether, like Bertrand Russell who, in *Why I am not a Christian*, never mentions it. So we conclude that in his case, at least, it is either because of ignorance or an example of 'running away from history'. [6]

So, judging from the example of Paul, one of the dominant needs for presenting the gospel to a pagan society, is to face people with the person of Christ and the evidence for the resurrection. There are, of course, other truths which are essential to salvation, and which will be included. But when approaching those who do not share our biblical presuppositions Luke shows from Paul's emphasis in Athens where we can begin. [7]

6

WHAT'S NEW?

The way that people react to the gospel does not necessarily tell us anything about the gospel, but it does reveal a great deal about them. It is similar to a person expressing his opinion about great works of art in an art gallery. If he declares that some of the paintings are not worth the canvas they are painted on, it is not likely to have any effect on their value. All his remarks succeed in doing is to reveal a lot about himself and his tastes, and he would probably be dismissed as an uncultured philistine.

So it is with response to the gospel. This is amply demonstrated in John's Gospel. The reaction of the Jews, for example, to the healing of the man born blind and the teaching connected with it in John 9, simply exposes their own spiritual condition as Jesus showed at the end of the chapter. Similarly we can add to our understanding of the people Paul encountered in Athens by observing the way they responded to him.

Luke first indicates the reaction of some of them to Paul himself: 'What is this babbler trying to say?' (Acts 17:18). This was not exactly an attractive way of referring to anyone. A 'babbler' or 'seed-picker' was a piece of Athenian slang, and denoted origi-

nally a bird that lived on seeds and odd scraps it
managed to scavenge from the streets. It came to be
used of a man who made money by posing as a
teacher of philosophy, but who had picked up his
scraps of learning from others. *The Good News Bible* renders it, 'What is this ignorant show-off trying
to say?' There seem to have been many of these people about, and some of them no doubt developed quite
a skill in concealing the second-hand nature of their
teaching and lack of any genuine knowledge.

Is this the familiar picture of people reading their
own faults into others? When I set out as a very young
minister a few years after the end of the war, a man
told me I was in the ministry only for what I could
'get out of it'. What I was in fact 'getting out of it'
was the princely sum of £250 a year after a long training and a university degree. It would buy much more
then before the inflation of the years that followed
but, as I had to pay everything out of it including
board and lodging, I did not feel particularly well-
off! But why did my critic make such a judgment
about my motives? Subsequent conversation revealed
all too clearly that 'what you get out of it' was his
only aim in life, and apparently he could not imagine that anyone could be different from himself. One
cannot help asking whether Paul's critics tacitly assumed that he had the same unworthy motives as
many of them.

In the same verse we encounter another reaction
showing their misunderstanding of Paul's teaching:
'He seems to be advocating foreign gods' – because

he preached Jesus and the resurrection. Just as people tend to see their own faults in others, so they will often read their own presuppositions into what they say. One way of doing this is to listen selectively, hearing what they agree with, and ignoring any ideas which are new to them. This seems to be how some of the Athenians grossly misunderstood what Paul was trying to convey to them. Although much that he said went over their heads, or was simply ignored through lack of interest on their part, they pricked up their ears whenever he referred to 'Jesus and the resurrection'. With their long tradition of polytheism it sounded to them like a personification of 'healing' and 'restoration', which is what 'Jesus' and 'resurrection' mean in Greek, and they assumed that Paul was introducing them to two new deities, perhaps a married couple! Paul and Barnabas had a similar experience with a pagan audience in Lystra, when they were regarded as incarnations of the gods, Zeus and Hermes.

This is a difficulty for which we must always be on the look-out, whenever we are speaking to people with deeply ingrained assumptions. A very common example is the assumption that if there is a God who gives any kind of salvation to men, then it must be as a reward for a good life. I have known this view to be read into a sermon which said precisely the opposite. On one occasion when this happened to me I had spoken on the text, 'It is by grace you have been saved, through faith – and this not from yourselves, it is the gift of God – not by works, so that no-one can boast' (Ephesians 2:8-9). I thought I had made it crystal clear that salvation is offered to us as a free gift from God by virtue of Christ's death on the cross, and is not earned by us. After the service a respectable looking lady told me what a wonderful sermon it was. My understandable pleasure at such a compliment was stifled at birth, however, when she added, 'It is just what my late husband used to say, do your best and God will reward you'!

Sometimes we can unwittingly court misunderstandings of this kind out of a genuine desire to make the gospel relevant to people by using their language. Some, when speaking against the background of the drug scene, have used expressions like 'getting high on Jesus'. This is tantamount to asking our hearers to read their own outlook into what we are saying with the possible result that they come to regard Jesus as a kind of drug. Many of the thought forms into which our message may well be interpreted relate to subjective experiences, because that is what many are seeking today. Commercial advertising is full of it. A brand of tobacco is 'cool and refreshing'; a certain drink is 'satisfying'; other products such as make-up, toothpaste and deodorants give 'confidence'; while others offer what promises to be 'exhilarating' or 'exciting'. So we need not be surprised if when we speak of guilt they will assume that we mean psychological guilt, rather than moral guilt before God, of which the Bible speaks. In this context, then, we must be careful not to over-emphasise the subjective results of being a Christian such as joy and peace, if we wish to avoid giving the impression that Christianity is just a piece of good psychology. After all what matters most of all is the fact of sins forgiven, more than any feelings resulting from it.

There is another observation that is worth making in passing. Paul's hearers were ready enough to adapt what he said to their preconceived notions, but they still regarded them as '*foreign* gods' (Acts 17:18). Now it has sometimes been maintained that the New Testament doctrine of the death and resurrection of Christ is a Christianised version of the Greek myth of the dying and rising again of the nature god. If this is so, why did the Athenians not recognise Paul's teaching as such? On the contrary, not only did they regard the gods they thought Paul was bringing them as foreign, but they also assumed that what he taught was '*new* teaching' (Acts 17:19), and that he was bringing '*strange* ideas' to their ears (Acts 17:20). This hardly suggests that the Athenians thought that Paul's message had anything in common with the death-and-rebirth myths of the mystery religions. We find Paul himself making the same observation. His preaching of the death of Christ, far from being recognised as part of a familiar pagan myth in another form was, as he put it, 'foolishness to Gentiles' (1 Corinthians 1:23).

Now it was the newness of Paul's teaching that proved to hold the special fascination for the Athenian mind which occasioned the delivery of the Areopagus address. It was a characteristic for which they were known, as Luke explains:

> All the Athenians and the foreigners who lived there
> spent their time doing nothing but talking about and
> listening to the latest ideas (Acts 17:21).

The Athenians had long been known for this. Professor F. F. Bruce has drawn his readers' attention to the Greek orator Demosthenes who, four hundred years earlier, had reproached them for going about asking if there was any fresh news in a day when Philip of Macedon's rise to power presented a threat which called for deeds not words. [1]

The disillusionment with what was traditional on the part of many in the Athens of Paul's day, might well have been an added reason for running after novelties.

This particular characteristic of the people of Athens is well worth reflection as we approach the end of the twentieth century. In Western countries such as the United States and Britain, the second half of the century has been marked by a decline in moral standards with tragic social and economic effects. Most commentators see what is often called 'the swinging sixties' as the decade in which the downturn took place. An interesting study of the revolution in British life which occurred during that period was made by Christopher Booker under the title, *The Neophiliacs*. This seems to have been a word specially coined for the purpose, presumably meaning, lovers of what is new. Although essentially a secular book, it contains biblical quotations and the author likens what he is describing to the Athenians of Acts 17. [2] Among the groups responsible for the far-reaching changes in the period covered by the book, the author discerns The Oxbridge 'Intellectuals' and the upper-class young about whom he comments:

> The upper classes in England had in fact been losing faith in their traditional values, and bourgeois self-confidence had been crumbling for over half a century. [3]

He then draws attention to 'the great upper-middle class swing to the left in the Thirties', as it was during that period that Oxford in particular produced the class rebels that led the search for a new freedom and vitality after the war, and which further led among other things to the cult of youth that grew up in the sixties.

So disillusionment with the traditions and values of the past may be one of the reasons common to the first and twentieth centuries for 'telling or hearing something new' (Acts 17:21, RSV). In Athens it may have been the inadequacies of popular religion which left a vacuum, while the dead formalities of nominal Christianity may have contributed to the situation today. At the same time, however, there is one very important difference. In ancient times little of any significance noticeably changed. As the years and even the centuries passed by, people wore the same clothing, travelled by the same means, lived in the same kind of houses and fought their wars with the same type of weapons. So the search for new ideas in philosophy and religion could not be said to arise out of changes in everything else.

With the twentieth century it is very different. One of the most prominent features of the past hundred years has been the way in which everything has been changing, and hardly any aspect of life has been exempt. Not only has the rate of change been breathtaking, but in recent years changes have accelerated out of all proportion. My attention to this phenomenon was drawn by Alvin Toffler who wrote:

> the world today ... is as different from the world in which I was born as that world was from Julius Caesar's. I was born in the middle of human history, to date, roughly. Almost as much has happened since I was born as happened before. [4]

This applies to science and technology, medicine, population growth and the using up of the world's energy resources. And the changes are accelerating. Of the many examples Toffler chooses there is speed of travel which has the advantage that it can be measured. In 1784, he reminds us, the first mail coach averaged a mere 10 mph. The first steam locomotive in 1825 made only a slight improvement on this by achieving a top speed of 13 mph. In the 1880s, however, the more advanced steam locomotives reached what then seemed an enormous speed – 100 mph – but it took the entire history of the human race to attain that record. Here is how Toffler continues the story:

> It took only fifty-eight years, however, to quadruple the limit, so that by 1938 airborne man was cracking

the 400 mph line. It took a mere twenty year flick of time to double the limit again. And by the 1960s rocket planes approached speeds of 4,800 mph, and men in space capsules were circling the earth at 18,000 mph. Plotted on a graph the line representing progress in the past generation would leap vertically off the page.

Whether we examine distances travelled, altitudes reached, minerals mined, or explosive power harnessed, the same accelerative trend is obvious. The pattern here, and in a thousand other statistical series, is absolutely clear and unmistakable. Millenia or centuries go by, and then, in our own times, a sudden bursting of the limits, a fantastic spurt forward.[5]

It is not surprising that in this kind of world people are constantly expecting something new. Luxuries soon cease to satisfy in the anticipation that they will shortly be surpassed by some fresh invention. Radio is no longer the novelty it once was since the arrival of television on the scene, and this in turn must have the various accessories which have been added to it. For many years clothing, for women at least, has constantly changed with new fashions every year. We live in what has come to be called a 'throw-away-society': of ballpoint pens which are discarded as soon as they run out, disposable towels, non-returnable bottles and even wrist watches which are replaced rather than repaired.

A few years ago I discovered that it applied also to computers. I took mine back to the dealer for servicing and minor repairs only to be told that he could not obtain spare parts because it was 'rather old-fashioned' – it was less than four years old! Although our washing machines, freezers, cameras and cars are fit to last for many years, commercial advertising is constantly persuading us that we need new ones and that there are better models on the market. And so we could continue with example after example of how modern man is being brainwashed into thinking that he must always be having 'something new'.

How is Christianity likely to be viewed by such a society? Will it hold out a fascination as yet something else that is new? Here, unfortunately perhaps, we have to face a difference between pre-Christian and post-Christian paganism. Today the gospel, rather than being greeted as one of the 'latest ideas', is more likely to be dismissed with the sarcastic quip, 'Tell me the old, old story'! Christianity, like so many other things, belongs to a past which has now been superseded, and every disused or little-used church building seems to confirm that this is so.

The way to attract interest in Christianity, it would seem, is to announce that one has discovered a new version which discards many of its traditional tenets. R. J. Campbell did it at the City Temple in London as the beginning of the twentieth century, the expected golden age of the secular optimists of those days, approached. He produced his so-called 'New Theology', and had a book published with that title. More recently John Robinson created a stir with his *Honest to God*. A few years ago I heard it suggested that the way a church leader can get publicity is to announce that he no longer believes in the resurrection, in saying his prayers or going to church. Why is it that the orthodox evangelical churches in British university towns, which are packed with students, are rarely mentioned in the media? I once heard a journalist explain that they have 'no news value'. Apparently, then, people are still like the Athenians who 'spent their time in nothing except telling or hearing some thing new' (Acts 17:21, RSV).

A fascination with novelties can, of course, provide openings for the gospel as it did for Paul and make people ready to discuss religion. There is, however, the danger of trifling with serious issues. This came home to me quite forcefully once when I was conducting a mission in a university. I was talking with one of the students who had responded to my invitation to seek help from a personal talk with me. As I seemed to be getting nowhere with him, I asked him why he had come to see me. He was perfectly frank. He was attending a short course in the Philosophy of Religion, and his tutor had recommended him to seek a personal interview with me, as he would find me an interesting subject for study. I was simply being regarded as a religious phenomenon! I suspect there was something of this in the Athenians' attitude to Paul. All this shows what an interesting subject religion can be, and why it is just the subject for an enjoyable discussion group, especially for those of whom Paul warned his young colleague, Timothy, who are 'always learning but never able to acknowledge the truth' (2 Timothy 3:7). Some will treat Christian truth like chewing gum, spending hours chewing it over in discussion, but never swallowing it.

Nevertheless it provided Paul with the kind of opportunity he was always ready to seize. It was through the Athenians' interest in the new ideas that Paul brought to their city that he was able to address the most distinguished academic audience of the day. So seeking for clarification, 'they took him and brought him to a meeting of the Areopagus, where they said to him, "May we know what this new teaching is that you are presenting? You are bringing some strange ideas to our ears, and we want to know what they mean" ' (Acts 17:19-20).

7

THE UNKNOWN GOD

The Court of the Areopagus took its name from the hill where it met, 'the hill of Ares', or 'Mars Hill' as the older English version renders it. It was in no sense a criminal court, but was a gathering of some of the leading minds of Athens, which had great influence and authority in matters of religion and morals. So to examine and pronounce on the new teaching brought by Paul was well within their terms of reference.

Paul began his discourse with an assessment of his hearers. This is always important for witness and evangelism in any setting. Paul's own advice is 'that you may know how to answer everyone' (Colossians 4:6). The observations he made during his stroll around the city suggested what his starting point should be. He first recognised that his hearers were basically religious, but in the same breath claimed that their religion was based on ignorance. He was able to substantiate his assessment by what he had seen in their city.

What an important principle this is! It is not enough to pour the truth into an unbelieving ear, no matter how skilfully it is done. There must be some understanding of our hearers, their problems and difficulties. This is why it is important to give the person we are seeking to help an opportunity to speak, if we are going to address ourselves to his or her need. As we saw in Chapter 4 this is one of the marks of the ministry of Jesus. He had a deep understanding of each individual who sought his help and, as a result had a different approach for each person. Here is one of the chief objections to stereotyped methods of approach, which map out the same entire conversation which the Christian is intended to have with anyone he is trying to win. True, it is necessary to have a clear grasp of the basic facts of the gospel which must be ultimately covered in leading a person to faith in Christ, but this is not the same as prescribing a detailed technique. If we are to start with people where they are, there is no line of approach which fits all cases, and there is no evidence that Paul or anyone else in the New Testament employed one either. This especially needs remembering when we are faced with people with no Christian background.

To return to Paul's first point, here is how he put it: 'Men of Athens! I see that in every way you are very religious' (Acts 17:22). This does not mean that they were 'religious' in the best sense of the word. F. F. Bruce has observed, 'This characterisation of the Athenians was not necessarily intended by Paul to be complimentary; the expression he used may also mean "rather superstitious".'[1] That is how the King James' Version renders it and it may well be that the Greek word covers both ideas in its range of meaning, referring to an awareness deeply ingrained in the human mind that there are powers other that physical.

This is the general assumption of the Bible. In the Old Testament it is only 'the fool' who 'says in his heart, "There is no God"' (Psalm 53:1). The writers of the New Testament make the same assumption that man has some religion, no matter how distorted or debased it is. Religion then is normal for the human race, whereas lack of it is abnormal.

Some have maintained the opposite, that it is religion that is abnormal, while lack of it is a sign of healthy normality. Freud regarded this supposed abnormality as a neurosis, which seeks to solve its problems by projecting on to an imagined God the desire for a father. It never seems to have occurred to him that his own lack of religion could be accounted for in similar terms, and arising out of the bad relationship he had suffered with his own father. Others have fastened on to the well-known statement by Karl Marx that religion is an opiate to keep the underprivileged masses content with their lot, which would suggest that it was invented by capitalists, although I have been told that there is evidence that Marx himself thought more deeply about religion than that.

It is, however, the Bible view that is borne out by evidence. There may be many individuals who profess to be atheists, but there has never been a race of men without belief in the supernatural, even if it has been nothing more than a primitive animism. Cicero once claimed, 'There is no nation so barbarous, no race so savage, as not to be fully persuaded of the being of God.' [2]

It must be because religion is so much part of

human nature, that years of militant atheism in the Soviet Union and other communist dictatorships, with all their senseless persecutions, failed to obliterate it from the minds of their people. It survived even in the mind of Svetlana, the daughter of the brutal Soviet tyrant, Joseph Stalin.

The same can be said of the way that people, when put under sufficient pressure, will feel for a God who has become their only hope. I once heard a former sailor speaking of his wartime experiences. He told of how, having been torpedoed, he spent some days in an open boat with a few of his comrades. Some of them had claimed to have renounced all religion, and had often sneered at his Christian profession giving him an uncomfortable time. Faced with the increasing likelihood of death, as the days passed by with no rescuer in sight and they gradually grew weaker, one of them eventually suggested that their Christian ship-mate might pray for them, and they all readily agreed. 'By the time we were rescued,' he concluded, 'there wasn't an atheist among us!'

Julian Huxley, a celebrated and avowed atheist, once made a somewhat unexpected and remarkable admission. It was that man functions better if he acts as though God is there. Here is Francis Schaeffer's comment:

> These thinkers are saying in effect that man can only function as man for an extended period of time if he acts on the assumption that a lie (that the personal God of Christianity is there) is true. You cannot find any deeper despair than this for a sensitive person. [3]

And this was Paul's assessment of Athens. In spite of the professed atheism of many of his hearers, all around him were expressions of a human awareness of a need for God, and the many idols were examples of their clumsy attempts to find him. And this brings us to Paul's second observation. Not only is he surrounded by indications that people are 'incurably religious', but he has spotted one particular altar whose inscription speaks volumes: 'to an unknown god'.

There were other such altars, such as one which has been discovered at Pergamum with its inscription, 'to unknown gods'. We need not concern ourselves with what the original intention behind their erection might have been. Perhaps it was to ensure that no god was overlooked. What is of interest to us is the use that Paul made of the one in Athens. He saw the irony of it. After filling every corner of the city with idols to every deity they could think of, they were still worshipping in ignorance. This is how he put it to them:

> For as I walked around and looked carefully at your objects of worship, I even found an altar with this inscription: TO AN UNKNOWN GOD. Now what you worship as something unknown I am going to proclaim to you (Acts 17:23).

It reminds us of how Jesus described Samaritan worship to one of its adherents: 'You Samaritans worship what you do not know' (John 4:22).

The rendering 'you worship as something unknown' is not an altogether happy one as it could imply that God is unknowable. This is the view expressed by the term 'agnosticism'. When the word was coined in 1869 by Thomas Henry Huxley, Julian Huxley's grandfather, to describe his own position, he alluded to this inscription found by Paul. An agnostic is not an atheist, who dogmatically asserts that there is no God, but describes someone who does not know whether God exists or not. Strictly it refers to the view that even if God and other spiritual phenomena exist, they cannot be known.

Now Paul would never have meant that. We have here a Greek present participle, which literally means, 'you worship not knowing'. Professor N. B. Stonehouse points to the true significance of this when he writes:

> The ignorance rather than the worship is thus underscored, and Paul is indicating that he will inform them with regard to that concerning which they acknowledge ignorance. [4]

According to him the NIV rendering (Stonehouse encountered it in the RSV):

> fails to make clear that Paul is characterising the *worshippers* as without knowledge rather than the object of the worship as being, from his own point of view, as such unknown.

So it was not a case that God could not be known, but rather that the Athenians had failed to find him.

This ignorance is even more striking when we recall the background against which Paul was speaking. He was not addressing uncivilised savages, but a community which, with some justification, took a pride in the quality of its intellectual life. Athens was an academic centre and could boast some illustrious names among its thinkers, such as Plato, Socrates and Aristotle, to mention three of the best known. Yet in spite of them all Paul still made his round assertion to a church in a Greek city, 'in the wisdom of God the world through its wisdom did not know him' (1 Corinthians 1:21).

It is natural to ask why this should be so. Why should the ancient Greeks, who numbered among them the great philosophers of the ancient world, make such poor progress in discovering the truth about God? And this was not the only field in which they failed to attain knowledge. Take for example chemistry. One view which was current among them was that everything comes ultimately from water. Another theory propounded by one of their philosophers was that air was the primary substance of the material world, while another philosopher came to the rival conclusion that fire was the fundamental principle. Finally there was the great Aristotle himself, who settled for four elements – earth, fire, air and water!

Malcolm Jeeves began a book about science and Christianity with this same question:

> Why did the Greeks, with all their magnificent intellectual and cultural achievements, fail to initiate and sustain the rise of science 2,000 years ago? Why did the scientific revolution begin in earnest in the sixteenth century and flourish from then onwards? [5]

And just to rub it in, the answer to the question about why the modern scientific movement was born in the sixteenth century, is that it was chiefly the result of the Reformation, when Christendom rejected Aristotle whose views had become orthodoxy during mediaeval times, in favour of a biblical way of thinking. [6]

Now why were these ancient Greek theories so wide of the mark? And why were the ideas of Aristotle such a hindrance to scientific progress? They never doubted that the universe is subject to laws and is therefore capable of explanation, and yet they made little progress in discovering it. Now of the reasons Professor Malcolm Jeeves advances for this, there is one which is of particular interest to us:

> Because the mind of man was rational, the Greeks elevated the process of intuition and the use of reason above careful observation. [7]

Jeeves then rounds off this point with a quotation from W. K. C. Guthrie: '... the philosophers tried to explain nature while shutting their eyes.' [8]

It was largely Sir Francis Bacon, in the seventeenth century, who persuaded scientific investigators to cease from 'shutting their eyes', so that explanations about the nature of matter began to be based on the experimental method. This is where modern developments in physics and chemistry had their birth.

This over-reliance on reason did not hinder the ancient Greeks from being competent pure mathematicians, but it was quite inadequate for discovering the facts of physics and chemistry. Perhaps this was also why Leibniz, in the seventeenth century, was both a philosopher and a mathematician. His rationalism served him well in sharing with Newton the discovery of the calculus, but his theory about what he called 'monads' as the basic substances of which the universe was supposed to consist, was not so enlightened.

The same can be said of ancient Greek attempts to find God. He is not found by speculation and philosophy, even when it is the mind of a Socrates or an Aristotle which is engaged in it. Nor, to express the same approach at a more popular level, is he to be found by wishful thinking. It may, for example, be a pleasant thought to imagine that God is love, but that in itself is no guarantee that it is true. 'I like to think ...', as some people introduce their religious opinions, is no basis on which to settle the deepest issues of life. It is no more, as we saw in Chapter 2, than a mental image, an idol in the mind. Surely if we have nothing better to rely upon than such do-it-yourself religiosity, whether or not we possess trained philosophical minds, none of us can hope to be anything other than agnostic or, to use the Latin equivalent of this basically Greek word, an 'ignoramus'!

Christianity offers something much better than unaided human speculation. It is that God has come to this earth in the person of Jesus Christ and revealed himself and his way of salvation. Paul could prove that from the Old Testament Scriptures which he and his fellow Jews had been brought up to believe to be inspired by God. That was all very well in the Jewish synagogues, as it is today with nominal Christians who respect the Bible as God's Word. But what about the pagans of Athens, who would have looked back in blank bewilderment if Paul had prefixed what he said with 'The Bible says ...'. And what do we say to those today who protest that they don't accept the divine authority of the Bible? Also, for that matter, what about Christians who are beset with doubts about the Bible's inspiration and authority?

I mention this because, as a young Christian, I had problems about the inspiration of the Bible. On one occasion, when I asked an older Christian, I was referred to 2 Timothy 3:16, a fine statement it is true, but it seemed to be a circular argument to use the Bible to prove the Bible! To make it worse I heard other Christians advance, as a reason for accepting the Bible, the peace and joy it had brought them. But I could not find unreliable feelings as a ground for belief among New Testament Christians. Paul, for example, spoke in Romans 15:13 (KJV and RSV) of 'joy and peace in believing' and not 'believing in joy and peace'.

So if Paul did not enforce any of his points with 'The Bible says...' what did he say instead? A year or two ago I read in some well-known evangelical Bible reading notes the following comment on the Areopagus address:

Paul spoke to them in their own terms. There were no

> references to the Old Testament; no-one would have understood them. *Instead* (italics mine) there were quotations from Greek poets (Epimenides and Aratus, verse 28), plus a more or less philosophical analysis of Greek thinking.

Now that Paul 'made no references to the Old Testament' and quoted Greek poets is plain for all to see. Also the writer proceeds to draw some helpful conclusions about the need for evangelism to be culturally sensitive. That is why it is important for us to understand the thinking of the world, to read its literature and be acquainted with what the media are feeding it with. In this respect Paul had an advantage similar to Moses who 'was educated in all the wisdom of the Egyptians' (Acts 7:22). But does this really mean that, after the way the apostle normally used the Old Testament in the synagogues, he quoted Greek poets 'instead'? I only hope that on the few occasions when I quote Shakespeare in the pulpit (it usually is Hamlet which I once did as a set book!) or some other piece of secular literature, no one concludes that I am quoting it 'instead' of Scripture. I hope it was a verbal slip on the writer's part, but I refer to it because it expresses a misunderstanding I have encountered before.

So how does Paul answer the agnosticism of those who neither know, nor accept the Bible? Note the claim he now sets before his hearers:

Whom therefore ye ignorantly worship, him declare I unto you (Acts 17:23, KJV).

I quote the King James' Version because of a further reason why I cannot accept the NIV. The latter renders it, 'I am going to proclaim to you'. But the Greek is a present tense and not a future, as though Paul is referring only to what he is about to say on Mars Hill. We have to remember that Paul was taken there to explain his ministry in the market-place, which had as its main emphasis, 'Jesus and the resurrection'. He might well have put it like this: 'When I argue that Jesus was more than a man, and tell you of the evidence for the resurrection, I am showing you grounds for believing in the existence and nature of God, whom you can find in no other way.'

We may indeed be unable to find God through the limitations of our minds, but God has come to us in the person of Jesus Christ and revealed himself through his incarnate life. How do I know that God is a Father, that he is righteous and that he loves his creatures? Is it because such ideas appeal to my reason or my feelings? That provides no ground for finite minds with changeable feelings to believe anything. No, the reason for believing these and other facts about God, is the discovery that God himself has disclosed them in the person and life of Christ.

But what about the authority with which Paul could quote from the Old Testament in a synagogue. How can he cope without that in pagan Athens? Here we must look at two important words which Paul employed. Firstly there is 'proclaim' (RSV) or 'declare' (KJV). It consists of a word commonly used for preaching the gospel: *angelo*, which means to make

an announcement. It often has the prefix, *eu* to show
that it is good news, and can be transliterated into
English by 'evangel', or translated into our native
equivalent, 'gospel'. Here in Acts 17 the prefix is
kata, giving a word which Professor Stonehouse
points out 'is used frequently in the Acts and Pauline
epistles of the official apostolic proclamation of the
gospel.' [9] He can cite a number of examples from
New Testament usage to illustrate his point. 'The
word of God' is 'proclaimed' by Paul and Barnabas
(Acts 13:5; 15:36; 17:13); 'the testimony of God'
(RSV) was 'proclaimed' to the Corinthians (1 Corinthians 2:1); along with many other instances which
could be cited. [10]

Coupled with the word 'proclaim' is the emphatic
personal pronoun 'I'. Here is another device for asserting apostolic authority, when the first person is
denoted by a pronoun instead of leaving it to be expressed by the ending of the verb. [11] What Paul is
doing then, is not only claiming that God had revealed himself to man in 'Jesus and the Resurrection',
but that he, Paul, is one of God's appointed witnesses
of these great events. He asserts this claim with equal
force elsewhere. When writing to the Corinthians he
supplies them with a list of witnesses of the resurrection and includes himself: 'Last of all he appeared
to me also' (1 Corinthians 15:8). So he regarded his
experience of Christ on the Damascus Road as a witness of the resurrection, and a qualification to call
himself an apostle: 'Am not I an apostle? Have I not
seen Jesus our Lord?' (1 Corinthians 9:1).

This was the qualification which the other apostles recognised between the Ascension of Jesus and Pentecost. Having been commissioned by Jesus as his chosen witnesses (Acts 1:8) they decided to fill the gap left by the defection of Judas Iscariot. Whether they were acting out of turn in doing this, and God's plan was to make up the number to twelve again by the inclusion of Paul, is a question which need not concern us now. What is relevant to us at this point is the criterion they observed in choosing a replacement. Of those who had been with them throughout the ministry of Jesus 'one of these must become a witness with us of his resurrection' (Acts 1:22). For this ministry they were specially chosen by God, as Peter explained to Cornelius:

> He was not seen by all the people, but by witnesses whom God had already chosen – by us who ate and drank with him after he rose from the dead (Acts 10:41).

It was through this apostolic testimony that Jesus himself expected Christians subsequent to the original apostles to believe. In his prayer for his disciples he prayed not for the existing ones who had been with him during his earthly ministry and were about to witness his resurrection, but 'also for those who will believe in me *through their word*' (John 17:20, RSV). And that includes all those from the first century until today, who have believed in Jesus through what they have read of him in the writings of the apostles in the New Testament.

To return to Paul, he clearly regarded himself as one of those apostles, one of the 'witnesses whom God had already chosen'. Just as the original apostles had been promised the Holy Spirit by Jesus to aid their memory and guide them into further truth which, at that time, they could not then 'bear' (John 14:26; 16:12-13), he too had received the gospel he preached by direct revelation from God, and had received recognition from the other apostles (Galatians 1:11-2:10).

So what does Paul teach us about the place of the Bible when presenting the gospel to complete pagans? To say that he did not confront them with the Bible is not an accurate picture. He certainly did not use proof texts from the Old Testament although, as we shall see, he gave a view of God strongly reminiscent of Old Testament teaching. But what about the New Testament? He certainly could not quote from it as we might today, for the obvious reason that it was not yet written. Yet at the same time there was a sense in which the Athenians *were* being exposed to the New Testament, in that the one who was addressing them was one of its inspired writers. And when Paul used the expression 'I proclaim' which, as we have seen, was used to denote the authoritative proclamation of an apostle, he was really claiming the same authority as he did for his teaching in the epistles when he maintained, 'what I am writing to you is the Lord's command' (1 Corinthians 14:37). This is how the Bible came about. 'Bibles were not rained down in a shower from heaven, some with

Apocryphas and some without.' [12] It was written by men who claimed a God-given authority.

It is with this that the unbelievers of every age must be confronted – the claims of the New Testament apostles. They may not regard their writings as inspired in the way that committed Christians do. Yet at the same time their claims concerning Jesus and his resurrection which, they insist, they witnessed, cannot be brushed aside lightly. They demand a verdict, whether in first century Athens with one of the apostles in person, or in the sophisticated world of the late twentieth century when we have to rely on their writings.

And we must not be afraid of doing it in a multifaith society. Lesslie Newbigin is clearly unhappy with his observation that 'when thinking of our unbelieving English neighbours we speak of evangelism; when speaking of our Asian and West Indian neighbours we speak of dialogue.' He adds 'It is a conclusion which the Asian Christians in our cities find exceedingly odd'.[13] Of course we must listen and understand our hearers and where they come from, as Paul did in Athens. But what is called for, whether addressing nominal Christians, those of other religions or no religion, is to present the apostolic proclamation like Paul who declared: 'What therefore you worship as unknown, this I proclaim to you' (Acts 17:23, RSV).

THE PERSONAL GOD

If, as Paul claimed, God has answered our natural ignorance about him by revealing himself through 'Jesus and the resurrection', our next question must surely be concerned with what God has shown himself to be like. Or, to pick up another thread from our last chapter, if Paul was one of God's chosen witnesses of the historical events concerning Jesus, and therefore able to assert with apostolic authority, 'this I proclaim to you,' what kind of a God was he in fact proclaiming to them?

Those who had seen Jesus in the flesh were expected to have learned something about God who was disclosing himself through him. This was the point of Jesus' reply to Philip in the upper room when he asked, 'Lord, show us the Father'. Jesus replied:

> 'Don't you know me, Philip, even after I have been among you such a long time? Anyone who has seen me has seen the Father. How can you say, "Show us the Father"? Don't you believe that I am in the Father, and that the Father is in me?' (John 14:8-10)

Yet there is no suggestion in the teaching of Jesus that he was revealing God for the first time. He constantly assumed that his Father was the God of the

Old Testament Scriptures. Paul too shared this pre-supposition, as he frequently indicated in his writings. And it was the nature and character of God as it is set forth in the Old Testament that Paul found confirmed in the person of Christ. Paul would have readily assented to the opening declaration of the epistle to the Hebrews:

> In the past God spoke to our forefathers through the prophets at many times and in various ways, but in these last days he has spoken to us by his Son, whom he has appointed heir of all things... (Hebrews 1:1-2)

In Athens, as we have already observed, Paul does not look to the Old Testament for proof texts. The truth of what he says rests upon the person and resurrection of Jesus. Nonetheless it is perfectly clear that it was the God of the Old Testament that Jesus had affirmed, and whom Paul was now proclaiming, and it was in Old Testament language that he naturally expressed himself. Look at how he begins: 'The God who made the world and everything in it ...' (Acts 17:24). Here is an unmistakable allusion to Exodus 20:11, where we find language which is repeated throughout the Old Testament. The same can be said of what follows: he 'is the Lord of heaven and earth and does not live in temples built by hands.' This recalls a sentence in Solomon's prayer at the dedication of the temple (1 Kings 8:27).

What then is one of the most distinctive features of the God of the Bible? It is that he is personal and has a particular relationship with his creatures. In this Paul corrects both extremes represented by the two schools of philosophy which he had encountered in the market-place, and which we briefly described in Chapter 4. To the Epicureans God, or the gods, having once created the world, had no further interest in it, and left it to the mercy of chance. For them God was unapproachable and unknowable, and so there was no prospect of any relationship with him. The Stoics, on the other hand, were pantheistic. That is, God was totally immanent in the world in the sense that there is nothing of him outside of it. He is its soul, so this also denies that God is a person with whom a relationship is possible.

The biblical revelation of God corrects both of these extremes. On the one hand God is transcendent, elevated above his creation. But this is not the whole truth about him. If it were, God would be beyond man's reach and therefore unknowable. In the Bible, however, this truth is balanced by another, equally essential: God is also immanent. So although quite distinct from the universe as a separate being, God is none the less constantly at work in it, directing it, sustaining it and operating the laws which he himself has established. Above all he has a special relationship with the human race, which enjoys a privileged status as the crown of creation. We find both of these emphases in the Bible, but perhaps no statement is clearer than the one in the prophet Isaiah which brings them together in perfect balance:

This is what the high and lofty one says –
  he who lives for ever, whose name is holy:
'I live in a high and holy place,
  but also with him who is contrite and lowly in spirit'
                                    (Isaiah 57:15).

Now it is this same balance of truth which the apostle maintains in his discourse to the Athenian leaders. He begins by stressing the transcendence of God and so provides a corrective to the Stoics. But he moves immediately to the close relationship which God holds with his creation, especially with man, articulating a truth which the Epicureans ignored.

The transcendence of God

Here Paul makes three basic points. To begin with he describes God as the Creator of 'the world and everything in it'. And this Creator is no intermediate being or Demiurge; he is 'the Lord of heaven and earth' (Acts 17:24a).

Secondly, his immensity forbids that he should be confined within man-made shrines (Acts 17:24b). We have already noted that this recalls something which Solomon said at the dedication of the temple. Isaiah made the same point:

This is what the LORD says:

  'Heaven is my throne,
  and the earth is my footstool.
Where is the house you will build for me?
  Where will my resting place be?'

                                    (Isaiah 66:1).

It was the recognition of this truth which led Stephen into trouble with the Jerusalem authorities. His defence was simply to reaffirm the inadequacy of any building, even Solomon's or Herod's temple, to house the eternal God, and he appealed to this same statement from Isaiah (Acts 17:47-49). Both he and Paul might have said to their respective hearers, in the words of J.B. Phillips' book title, 'Your God is too small'.

Paul's third point is to stress the self-sufficiency of God: 'And he is not served by human hands, as if he needed anything' (Acts 17:25a). Men are not required to worship God because he cannot do without it, as though he were an inadequate and insecure personality who needs constant confirmation of his greatness and who hungers after admiration. Here is another distortion which the Old Testament opposed (e.g. Psalm 50:9-12). In fact it is quite the opposite, 'because he himself gives all men life and breath and everything else' (Acts 17:25b). In other words far from God needing us, it is we who need him.

It is worth mentioning the importance to science of this stress on a transcendent Creator. The confusion of God with creation made true science impossible. It could take the form of idolatry in which God is conceived of in material terms. Or it could be animism which assumes that natural effects are produced by spirits. If a chemical reaction, such as the effervescence that results when an acid is added to chalk, is simply a spirit at work, then there is no place for scientific questions to be asked. Pantheism, which was popular among many of Paul's hearers, had a similar effect. Belief in the transcendence of God, however, leaves room for secondary causes to operate, which is the realm investigated by science. According to one interpretation those supernatural forces, belief in which delayed the rise of science, are the 'elemental spirits' which Paul was referring to when he wrote:

> When we were children, we were slaves to the elemental spirits of the universe. But when the time had fully come, God sent forth his Son ... so that we might receive adoption as sons (Galatians 4:3-5).

Lesslie Newbigin has described this reference to the breakthrough, which resulted from God's full revelation through the coming of Christ, as the New Testament's 'own account of man's coming of age'. [1]

It was of course many centuries before biblical teaching was given the opportunity to open the door to the rise of the scientific movement. When it did it is hardly surprising that a high proportion of pioneers in science were committed Christians, sometimes ordained ministers. They were compelled by a firm belief that the world around them was operated by rational laws which had been devised by the Creator who had made himself known through the Bible. As C. S. Lewis has remarked,

> Men became scientific because they expected Law in Nature, and they expected Law in Nature because they believed in a Legislator. [2]

It is not surprising that scientific papers were often headed by a text from the Bible, while the Cavendish Laboratory in Cambridge, Britain, has a verse from the Bible over its entrance.

Today has witnessed a decline in belief in a personal God. Modern scientific man has to a large extent decided to shake off the beliefs to which he has owed so much. Is it not significant that this has been accompanied by a growth in superstition, a revival in astrology and a turning to other unscientific ideas? And this is taking place in Western countries which have stood to gain most from the progress of science. The trouble is that there are still questions which must be asked and which science can never answer. If they have lost all knowledge of a personal Creator, where else is there to turn? Lesslie Newbigin concludes:

> Questions about personal destiny, about the meaning and purpose of human life, will always be asked, whatever the umpires of the language game may say. If there is no doctrine of divine providence then the vacuum will be filled by some kind of belief in luck, in fate or in the stars. [3]

The immanence of God

Paul also had to correct the opposite error of the Epicureans, who believed that God was solely transcendent, and had left the world to chance. Early progress in science led in the eighteenth century to the same extreme, usually known as deism. The main difference was that, instead of leaving the universe to chance, it was supposed that God had left it to be operated by the laws he had established. So impressive did these laws which were being discovered appear to be, that it seemed that once God had created the universe, he was no longer needed. The laws of nature were sufficient to maintain creation without any further divine intervention or providence. God has sometimes, according to this theory, been likened to a watchmaker who has made a watch which, once it has been wound up, will continue to run without any further maintenance. No salvation can be expected from such a God, nor is prayer of any avail, because he cannot be reached. Our lives are determined by impersonal, mechanistic forces. This falls hopelessly short of the personal God known to Christians.

All this represents the other extreme which the apostle was out to correct. But God has left creation neither to the mercy of chance, nor to the autonomy of the laws which he has devised. Instead he is very much involved in the world and especially in the affairs of men. In stressing the immanence of God Paul makes four points.

Firstly, not only did God create all things, but he is the Lord of all that he has made (Acts 17:24). This does not sound much like a God who has abandoned everything to chance or to a set of mechanical laws. Instead, as Paul's second point maintains, God sustains the human race and 'gives all men life and breath and everything else' (Acts 17:25b). Paul illustrates this by his quotation in verse 28 of the Greek poet, Epimenedes: 'In him we live and move and have our being'. Far from being directed by chance or impersonal laws, we depend on a living God for our life, activity and existence.

Next God orders human affairs so that migrations are caused neither by chance nor fate:

> From one man he made every nation of men, that they should inhabit the whole earth; and he determined the times set for them and the exact places where they should live (Acts 17:26).

Claims to territory are notorious as causes of bloodshed between nations and tyranny by despots. But as John Stott points out, 'both the history and geography of each nation are ultimately under his control'.[4]

Paul's fourth assertion of God's immanence reaches the heart of it: 'though he is not far from each of us' (Acts 17:27c). Here again is a truth frequently stressed in Scripture. We have, for example, Psalm 139 with its extensive statement of God's presence everywhere throughout creation (see especially verses 7-12). The prophet Jeremiah gives us another of the great sayings about the inescapable presence of God, whose nearness is as penetrating and searching at the farthest reaches of the universe as it is where one is standing now[5]:

> 'Am I only a God nearby,'
> > declares the LORD,
> 'and not a God far away?
> Can anyone hide in secret places
> so that I cannot see him?'
> > declares the LORD.

'Do not I fill heaven and earth?'
> declares the LORD
> (Jeremiah 23:23-24).

In speaking of the immanence of God, Paul has introduced yet another crucial theme with far-reaching implications – the Bible view of man. And this will not surprise us, because a person's perception of God will lead inevitably to a corresponding view of man. In general it may be said that a low or degraded view of God will involve a similar attitude to man. We can see this working out in the pagan society of Paul's day, where a very low value was placed on human life. There was widespread cruelty, especially in the treatment of slaves and prisoners of war, and even children were often ill-treated without question. To the superior Athenians non-Greeks were inferior. But when Paul introduced the Greeks to the personal God who had made himself known through Christ, and who is both transcendent and immanent, they also found themselves faced with a far more uplifting view of human worth.

This is reminiscent of a striking example in the Old Testament of an awareness of the worth of man coming in the context of these two fundamental doctrines of the relationship of God to his creation. It is a psalm which begins by viewing with awe and wonder the transcendent glory of God in creation. As the psalmist passes on to recall that this same God cares providentially for men, he finds himself compelled to ask, 'What is man?'

When I consider your heavens,
  the work of your fingers,
the moon and the stars,
  which you have set in place,
what is man that you are mindful of him,
  the son of man that you care for him?

                              (Psalm 8:3-4).

To this biblical doctrine of man, and its challenge to a pagan society, we must now devote ourselves.

9

GOD'S OFFSPRING

One of the characteristics of our present pagan society is an increasingly secular view of man. It is a view which regards him as nothing more than a body. Even the highest experiences of his life, his emotions, thoughts, opinions, morality and appreciation of art and beauty, are to be accounted for solely in terms of electrical impulses in the brain and nervous system and chemical changes in his glands. He is, in short, a complex organic machine and no more.

We ought to be under no illusions as to what this does to our attitude to life and to the effects of science, if we follow it through to its logical conclusion. Robert Brow acknowledges his indebtedness to C. S. Lewis when he writes:

> Science atomises and destroys every worthwhile thing that it looks at. A loved one becomes proteins and electrical impulses. Music is just vibrations. Responsibility vanishes into causes and effects. [1]

Science need not lead us to this sad state of affairs. There are many taking the lead today in various scientific fields who would strongly dissociate themselves from such a view. They would be as ready as any to study the way in which the body – including the brain – functions, and the part its processes play in the highest of our experiences. But they would stop short of claiming that this is the whole story. Science, they may put it, tries to answer the question 'how?' but is not equipped to answer the deeper question 'why?'. When, however, science is isolated from a spiritual view of man, then the accusation of Robert Brow sticks.

Of course people often resist the logic of their position and it is a mercy that they do. Church-goers have sometimes been accused of this kind of inconsistency, laying aside practical Christianity when they take off their Sunday clothes. Does a materialistic scientist do something similar when he takes off his lab' coat? Or does he really treat his wife and children as complex arrangements of protein molecules, and their emotions and feelings of love as nothing more than functions of their glands? Or what is perhaps more to the point, is he happy for them to treat him in the same way? Emil Brunner made the following comment about those who promote such materialist views:

> We all feel there is something distinctive about man, that he belongs to a 'higher' category than the rest of creation. Even the cynic who denies this in theory does not allow himself to be classified as an animal without protest, and he also expects other people to treat him in a 'human' fashion. Even when he expatiates upon his nihilistic views, in which he pours ridicule upon this 'distinctive' element in man, he demands a hearing as one who proclaims valid, absolutely valid truth

– an attitude which is not very fitting for a being who is nothing more than a 'degenerate cerebrating animal'. No man is a cynic where his own claim to be considered is concerned. [2]

Now it is questions like these which arise when we search for a basis for morality while retaining the presuppositions of materialism. Those who see themselves as progressives will not shrink from making moral judgments about capitalists who exploit the underprivileged, governments which follow racist policies, and detect all kinds of unworthy motives in the 'hypocrites' who stand for traditional sexual morality. It is not our purpose to take exception to these moral judgments, but to ask on what grounds a materialist can make them. Can a materialist tell me why, if I get the opportunity, I shouldn't steal his watch? After all it is only a process in my physical brain that moves my hand to pick it up when he isn't looking, and that process itself has taken place only because my mind has been predisposed that way by previous experiences. And what right have those with such views to pose as champions of humanity? Lunn and Lean have no doubt about the answer:

> If man be nothing but a collection of atoms every movement of which, including the movements which are alleged to generate thought, is the product of material causes, it is as absurd to accuse a man of inhumanity for erupting cruelty, as to accuse a volcano of inhumanity for erupting lava. [3]

And then, what about racism? If human beings are

no more than highly intelligent animals, why shouldn't the white variety, if it finds itself head of the jungle, maintain its position there?

But some progressives will in certain circumstances lay all moral judgments to one side! This they do when speaking of criminals and delinquents who, they say, are the helpless victims of their background, which has conditioned their behaviour. They really cannot help it. So in their case wrongdoing is not a sin that deserves to be punished, but a sickness that needs to be pitied. Moral judgments are to be reserved only for those who stand in the way of their 'progressive' views!

Admittedly when we are dealing with deranged minds who, by reason of illness, behave in an undesirable fashion, there are factors which must be taken into account. And the line where responsibility for our deeds begins is not always easy to draw. The trouble is that some don't want to draw any line at all, and imagine that to succeed in explaining wrong-doing is the same thing as excusing it. One cannot resist the suspicion that this is why some find these views so attractive. They relieve a person of any need to face moral problems in his or her life. Sins can be explained away in psychological jargon that takes away all responsibility. It is a sophisticated version of the schoolboy's innocent protest, 'Please Sir, it wasn't my fault.' But it is a degraded view of anyone to deny him responsibility for his actions, and it is hardly likely to do him much good. As usual Lunn and Lean ask the right questions:

The doctrine is put forward on compassionate grounds. But is it compassionate to tell people that they cannot help committing crime? Does this fill a weak man with hope and resolution? Or does it encourage him in the illusion that resistance to temptation is useless? [4]

Furthermore there are other ideas degrading to man which arise in materialistic circles. Sir Julian Huxley and other biologists, whose limited view of man has shaped the outlook of many during the twentieth century, have suggested that the human race can be improved by controlled selective breeding, thus reducing human beings to the level of farm animals. It is easy on this basis to appreciate that there can be little objection to destroying unborn babies, whose presence in the world would not be welcomed by whoever has succeeded in gaining the right to make decisions in such matters. After all they are only little biological machines. And then what about old people who can no longer make any useful contribution to human society? Is there any reason why they should take up space in old people's homes and the geriatric wards of our hospitals and waste the time of potentially useful humans who have to look after them? Why preserve life anyway? It is basically no more than a complicated protein molecule which we shall one day produce in a test tube. So perhaps the deeds of the Nazis ...

The materialistic view of man we have been considering is often referred to as humanism. But is this a suitable name? Would not sub-humanism be more fitting? Lunn and Lean recognised the contradiction in terms by entitling the chapter from which we have quoted, 'The inhumanity of the humanists'.

It could be objected with some justification that the description we have given of the secular view of man, and its logical outworking, has been far too brief to do justice to the important issues it raises. Also our treatment has left a high proportion of unanswered questions. Our purpose, however, is to show the predicament in which modern man finds himself. On a secular basis there are no answers to these questions. This is undoubtedly why this century has seen an increasing number of thinking people come to the conclusion that life is meaningless, and see no alternative to utter despair. As a young agnostic once put it to me shortly before he became a Christian, 'I have been persuaded by my friends to give up the outlook of my nominal Christian background. But as I have pursued this to its logical conclusion, I have succeeded in debunking every value in life, and I don't think it is worth living any more.'

Now Paul encountered something which was basically the same in Athens, especially among his Epicurean hearers. As Blaiklock described their views:

It was materialism thorough and absolute. The soul and mind, according to Democritus, was atomic in structure, atoms round and mobile, and infinitely subtle. Sight, hearing, taste, were the impinging of atoms on the senses, themselves material in structure. [5]

And Paul had something very positive to say to them to counter their low view of man. He maintained that

Christian revelation not only shows some important truths about God, but also gives an insight into the nature of man. The most important point about man concerns his special relationship to God: ' "In him we live and move and have our being." As some of your own poets have said, "We are his offspring" ' (Acts 17:28).

The Greek poets whom Paul was quoting, as he himself must have fully realised, meant something very different by these words from what he was teaching. Their view was a mystical pantheism which had little in common with what Paul believed. Nevertheless he found that these poets provided him with highly suitable language with which to express what was in his mind. Had he been addressing a Jewish audience on this theme we need only one guess as to what he would have quoted from the Old Testament:

> Then God said, 'Let us make man in our image, in our likeness' .... So God created man in his own image, in the image of God he created him (Genesis 1:26-27).

In making this statement about man's special relationship to his Creator, the biblical account of creation does not ignore that man possesses a material body, nor that he is involved with the animal world. In Genesis 2:7 Adam was both made from dust and also had the breath of life breathed into him by God which constituted him 'a living being'. Derek Kidner has summarised it as follows:

In both the opening chapters of Genesis man is portrayed as *in* nature and *over* it, continuous with it and
discontinuous. He shares the sixth day with other creatures, is made of dust as they are (2:7,19), feeds as
they feed (1:29,30) and reproduces with a blessing
similar to theirs (1:22, 28a); so he can well be studied
partly through the study of them: they are half his context. [6]

So we are not surprised that in our laboratories
medicine and surgery are tried out first on animals.
Nor need we be upset when psychology studies the
behaviour of animals and their learning process, and
applies its findings to man. His higher nature possesses and works by means of a highly developed
animal brain and nervous system.

Yet at the same time, between man and animals
there is a big divide. Emil Brunner once summarised
the differences like this:

The animal possesses understanding, no doubt, but no
reason. It has, no doubt, the beginning of civilisation,
but no culture. It probably has curiosity and knows
many things, but it has no science, it probably plays
but it has no art. It knows herds, but not fellowship. It
probably fears punishment, but has no conscience. It
probably realises the superiority of man, but it knows
nothing of the Lord of the World. [7]

It is this distinctness of man from the animals
that the Bible stresses. Man is presented as the crown-
ing phase in God's creation. He appears last on the
scene with all God's previous creative activity lead-

ing up to his creation. Of the rest of creation God simply says 'let us make', and there follows a bare command. Before the creation of man, however, there is a pause for counsel within the Godhead. Although the word 'create' is used sparingly in the rest of the story, in the case of man it is used no less than three times.

The most striking thing that the Bible says about man, however, is that he was created 'in the image of God'. This is a considerable advance on the way in which the animals appeared, they were simply brought forth 'according to their kinds'. So if a man is willing to look not only downwards upon the animal creation, but also upwards towards God, it is here that he will find what distinguishes him most fundamentally from the rest of creation. And it is this that makes man all that he is, 'Thinker, artist, scientist, builder; above all worshipper.' [8] Once this spiritual understanding of man is in place, we can safely make use of the various fields of human enquiry. As Emil Brunner commented on this phrase, 'the image of God',

> The first thing said about man in the Bible is that his relation to God is like that of a picture to its model. Man must first of all be defined theologically; only then may the philosopher, the psychologist and the biologist make their statements.[9]

How does all this affect our view of humanity? It surely imparts to it a dignity far greater than humanism can ever afford, and at the same time gives a sanctity to his life. One of the first deductions made in the Bible from this doctrine of the image of God, concerns the sanctity with which human life is to be regarded. Here is how it is expressed without going into all the issues raised:

> Whoever sheds the blood of man, by man shall his blood be shed; for in the image of God has God made man (Genesis 9:6).

James applied it even to the way we may speak to each other. We are not, he says, to 'curse men, who have been made in God's likeness' (James 3:9).

The biblical view of man accounts for why he is a moral being. Although many of Paul's converts had been rescued from lives of debauchery and corruption, he is quite prepared to admit that many Gentiles lived according to the last six of the ten commandments. Many of the Greek philosophers were great moralists, such as Seneca, the Stoic moralist and contemporary of Paul. F. F. Bruce draws attention to him among his comments on Romans 2.[10] There Paul is considering the spiritual standing of Gentiles who have not had the privilege of knowing God's law as the Jews had, and he concedes that

> when Gentiles, who do not have the law, do by nature things required by the law, they are a law for themselves, even though they do not have the law, since they show that the requirements of the law are written on their hearts, their consciences also bearing witness, and their thoughts are now accusing, now even defending them (Romans 2:14f).

The link between morality and being made in God's image must have been in the apostle's mind when he called on his readers 'to put on the new self, created to be like God in true righteousness and holiness' (Ephesians 4:24). So without discussing all that Paul is saying there, it is enough to note that being 'like God' (i.e. in his image) has to do with 'righteousness and holiness'. That men and women, then, are moral beings stems from their unique relationship with God. But it is in the parallel passage in the letter to the Colossians that we have what is surely the greatest of all the privileges arising out of being in God's image. It is that of being intended for the knowledge of God (Colossians 3:10).

How important it is for Christians, when surrounded by a non-Christian humanism that cannot but degrade man, to lay full stress on his true greatness! The danger is that, in our rightful concern to draw attention to man's depravity as a sinner, we lose sight of the dignity with which God has endowed him. Of course we must recognise the plight of man, and the desperate condition out of which he needs Christ as his Saviour. At the same time, however, God has invested him with great glory, as the psalmist long ago recognised:

> You made him a little lower than the heavenly beings
> and crowned him with glory and honour.
> You made him ruler over the works of your hands;
> you put everything under his feet (Psalm 8:5-6).

When Paul described man then as 'God's off-spring', these are the kind of thoughts that his Old Testament upbringing would have left at the back of his mind. He may have covered some of the points we have made, although he actually spelt them out in the epistles we have quoted, which were addressed to church members and not to unconverted Gentiles. Luke, however, does mention two aspects of human life which arise from Paul's doctrine of man, as the word 'for' at the beginning of verse 28 indicates. One is social and concerns human relationships, and the other religious and has to do with man's relationship to God.

He begins in verse 26 with a statement which is fundamental to human relationships. It is about the unity of the human race:

> From one man he made every nation of men, that they should inhabit the whole earth.

Here is Paul's answer to racism. This was an issue in first century Athens whose citizens were inveterate racists. Everyone was divided into two racial classes – Greeks and Barbarians. The Athenians made a further division – themselves and other Greeks, for they regarded themselves as true sons of the soil, not having migrated there as had the other inhabitants of the country.

In opposition to this, Paul was asserting that everyone comes from the same origin and all are of common stock, and this took from the Athenians, and anyone else for that matter, all grounds for racial

superiority. In view of Paul's background we might
well ask whether he had a clean bill of health himself in this matter. After all his Jewish compatriots
were hopelessly infected with a strong racial spirit,
referring as they did to 'Gentile dogs'. Paul, however, had moved a long way from that attitude which
he had come to recognise as one of the heresies of
contemporary Judaism. When God singled out Abraham and made promises to him and his descend-
ants, it was not to make them into a master race.
Rather it was to use them as the starting point from
which to bring the blessings of the gospel to the whole
world. The Old Testament prophets looked forward
to the Church of God ceasing to be a nation and becoming a world-wide multinational body. In contrast
to the racist attitude of the Jews, Paul maintained
that 'those who believe are children of Abraham' (Galatians 3:7). And he proceeded to explain that this
includes Gentile believers on the basis of God's prom-
ise to Abraham, 'All nations will be blessed through
you' (Galatians 3:8).

Jewish prejudice found this difficult to accept and
even Jewish Christians, including Peter, had to be
convinced. It was over this issue that Paul found himself in conflict with the Jews in Jerusalem, and they
arrested him because he 'brought Greeks into the
temple area' (Acts 21:28c). But Paul had good reason for treating the Gentiles with equality. As he was
later to explain to the Ephesians, in Christ the divid-
ing wall between Jew and Gentile has been broken
down. Both are reconciled to God on the same terms,

'through the cross' (Ephesians 2:16) and so,

> There is neither Jew nor Greek, slave nor free, male nor female, for you are all one in Christ Jesus (Galatians 3:28).

But it is not only within the Church that racial barriers are to be removed. It applies to the entire human race, because it is demanded not only by redemption, but also by the doctrine of creation. So Paul has a social message for the Athenians. There are, then, two reasons for rejecting racism which are brought together by Professor F. F. Bruce:

> Neither in nature nor in grace – neither in the old creation nor in the new – is there any room for ideas of racial superiority. [11]

This doesn't mean that all racial differences are to be overlooked, or that it is a Christian aim to merge our different cultures into a world-wide sameness. Nor ought we to pretend that we are colour blind, any more than the above quotation from the letter to the Galatians means that we ignore the differences between men and women. That we are not all the same adds a richness to human life. In matters of race as well as gender we may well say, 'Vive la différence!' Again the teaching of Scripture does not discourage a love for one's country and a concern for its well-being. It was permissible for the Jews to long for their country to be freed from the occupying Roman power, just as their forebears had sung about the plight of their country during the Babylonian exile centuries earlier: 'By the rivers of Babylon we sat and wept, when we remembered Zion' (Psalm 137:1).

Some have tried to distinguish between what is desirable and what is wrong by using two separate words, patriotism and nationalism. The value of the former has been shown by Lecky when he wrote in his *History of European Morals*:

> Patriotism leads men to subordinate their wishes to interests of the society in which they live. It extends the horizon of life, teaching men to dwell among the great men of the past, to derive their moral strength from the study of their heroic lives, to look forward continually, through the vistas of a distant future, to the welfare of an organisation which will continue when they have passed away.[12]

Nationalism, on the other hand, can be used to denote a very different spirit. Richard Aldington distinguished the two:

> Patriotism is a lively sense of collective responsibility. Nationalism is a silly cock crowing on its own dung-hill.[12]

It is perhaps worth noticing that this was written in 1938, when there were ugly examples of nationalism in Europe fed by racism. But a Christian's patriotism can be like Paul's in the deep concern he had for the spiritual needs of his fellow countrymen when he declared: 'Brothers, my heart's desire and prayer to God for the Israelites is that they may be saved' (Romans 10:1).

This brings us to the religious implication of man's special relationship to God. It arises from the way God has ordered his life on earth.

> That they should inhabit the whole earth; and he determined the times set for them and the exact places where they should live (Acts 17:26b).

Paul then explains that 'God did this so that men should seek him...' (verse 27). What exactly then did God do?

'The times set for them and the exact places where they should live' could be taken together to refer to the rise and fall of nations. In that case Paul is saying that God has ordered human history, which is, of course, in keeping with Old Testament teaching. One of its key statements is 'When the Most High gave the nations their inheritance, when he divided all mankind, he set up boundaries for the peoples...' (Deuteronomy 32:8). And if we wonder about who has the final say in the struggles for power through invasions and civil wars, the answer is found in God's reminder to Nebuchadnezzar when he had been congratulating himself on his attainments. The chastening in store for him was to be 'until you acknowledge that the Most High is sovereign over the kingdoms of men and gives them to anyone he wishes' (Daniel 4:32).

There is, however, a further point that Paul could be making here. It is possible that 'the times set for them' refers to the seasons of the year which make possible the seed time and harvest which are so vital for the provision of our needs. The actual tense of 'he determined' (RSV: 'having determined') implies that the earth was arranged in this way before man appeared on the scene, so that everything was ready to provide for him. This brings to mind what Winston Churchill said in his famous 'iron curtain' speech at Fulton, Missouri in 1946. Quoting Bourke Cochrane he asserted:

> There is enough for all. The earth is a generous mother: she will provide in plentiful abundance food for all her children, if they will cultivate her soil in justice and peace.

Paul's worldview is one that is obviously demanded today. Narrow nationalism and unthinking patriotism will not solve the most pressing problems facing the human race, such as the limited supply of energy, the shortage of food, the growth of the world's population and pollution. There is no master race, but 'every nation of men' has been made 'to inhabit the whole earth' under the Lord of seasons and history. It is urgent today that the human race views itself in these terms.

But Paul is drawing attention to another reason God had for so ordering our affairs and supplying our needs. He 'did this so that men should seek him...' (verse 27). It is not surprising that Paul made this point even more clearly in Lystra where he was addressing an agricultural community. There he attributed God's material provision to his kindness when he reminded them that he

> has not left himself without testimony: he has shown kindness by giving you rain from heaven and crops in their seasons; he provides you with plenty of food and fills your hearts with joy (Acts 14:17).

If man is God's offspring on whom he has bestowed his fatherly care, it would seem natural that man will be concerned to find his paternal Creator. Paul affirms that God himself expects this of us, and has arranged that we may find him. This he has done by leaving evidence of his activity in nature, as Paul indicates in the opening chapter of the Roman epistle:

> Since the creation of the world God's invisible qualities – his eternal power and divine nature – have been clearly seen, being understood from what has been made, so that men are without excuse (Romans 1:20).

In spite of this, man has not found his Creator. This is very clearly implied in the Areopagus address. The word 'reach' in verse 27 ('feel', KJV, RSV) is used both in classical Greek and in the Septuagint for groping in the dark. The word 'though' is also significant, as Stonehouse has detected:

> The concessive character of this statement indeed confirms the conclusion that the goal of finding God has not been attained. [13]

So people grope after God like blind men even

though he is not far from any of us. The various man-made religions in the world represent the quest for God and for a meaning to life. Today there is a surfeit of them. In addition to the historic world religions, there is a variety of sub-Christian sects and extreme cults with their techniques in personality domination. The latest arrival on the scene is the complicated mixture of pantheism, mysticism, astrology and other beliefs which make up the New Age movement.

To Paul there was one outstanding piece of evidence that men had not found God. It was the prevalence of idolatry of which he had found many examples in Athens. He explains this in the first chapter of Romans in what follows the verse we have quoted:

> Their thinking became futile and their foolish hearts were darkened. Although they claimed to be wise they became fools and exchanged the glory of the immortal God for images made to look like mortal man and birds and animals and reptiles (Romans 1:21b-23).

Now to Paul this just will not do for man with his privileged relationship with God, as he proceeds to point out:

> Therefore since we are God's offspring, we should not think that the divine being is like gold or silver or stone – an image made by man's design and skill (Acts 17:29).

This applies not only to those who bow down to idols of wood and stone. As we saw in Chapter 2 there were those in Athens, as in the present day, who have their mental images of God. These are nothing more than the product of their imagination of what they would like God to be. As a result all they have is an 'unknown god'. But as Paul insists, for man to fail to know God whose offspring he is, is a contradiction of one of the supreme purposes of his creation. Little wonder that the life of so many falls far short of what God intended. Because we are God's offspring, created in his image, in the time-honoured words of Augustine, 'Thou hast made us for thyself, and our hearts are restless till they find their rest in thee.'

10

GOD'S DEMAND

So far Paul had probably been well received. He clearly knew how to address a sophisticated audience. He gave them a balanced statement of spiritual truth in well chosen language. He revealed his understanding of his hearers by quoting from their literature. In fact his address could have passed muster as a university sermon! There were fresh ideas, it is true, but this would not have bothered the Athenians who were not averse to novelty. Nor would many of them have taken exception to his criticism of idolatry, as most of the more refined intellects among them felt the same.

Any favourable impression, however, that Paul may have created must have been brought to an abrupt end by what he said next: 'In the past God overlooked such ignorance, but now he commands all people everywhere to repent' (Acts 17:30).

Sophisticated intellects who enjoy having their fancies tickled by novel ideas, don't usually take kindly to appeals to commitment. A religion that provides an interesting topic for an evening's discussion is quite acceptable, but not anything that demands a response. The word 'repent' is not the kind of language for polite society that resents being preached at.

Professor Blaiklock suggests that the reactions of the two groups of philosophers would have been somewhat different:

> The Epicureans had listened impatiently throughout. They were those who scoffed. The Stoics dismissed him with more polite formality. The true Stoic, the Wise Man of their famous concept needed no repentance, feared no Day of Judgment, looked for no resurrection or reward. [1]

Of what Blaiklock calls the 'psychology of rejection', he has found a telling description by C. S. Lewis:

> We who defend Christianity find ourselves constantly opposed not by the irreligion of our hearers, but by their real religion. Speak about beauty, truth and goodness, or about a God who is simply the indwelling principle of these three, speak about a great spiritual force pervading all things, a common mind of which we are all parts, a pool of generalised spirituality to which we can all flow, and you will command friendly interest. But the temperature drops as soon as you mention a God who has purposes and performs particular actions, who does one thing and not another, a concrete, choosing, commanding, prohibiting God with a determinate character. People become embarrassed and angry. [2]

This was the reaction Paul encountered in Athens when his audience discovered that the God of which he was speaking makes moral demands of his creatures. Yet this ought hardly to have surprised them.

If man is God's offspring, and created in his image, then we must expect God to treat him as a morally responsible being.

It is at this point in Paul's address that we encounter the age-old problem about the eternal prospects of those who have never heard the gospel. This could well have been especially acute in Athens with ancient philosophers like Socrates, who possessed many commendable qualities, but lived before the coming of Christ. Paul said that 'in the past God overlooked such ignorance' (KJV: 'winked at'), and something similar at Lystra: 'In the past, he let all nations go their own way' (Acts 14:16). But he seems to have said something very different to his Roman readers when he assured them that 'since creation God's invisible qualities – his eternal power and divine nature – have been clearly seen, being understood from what has been made ... men are without excuse' (Romans 1:20). So what are we to make of this apparent contradiction? F. F. Bruce provides a pointer to the most likely explanation:

> There is, of course, a difference of emphasis, for there he is writing to established Christians and here he is trying to gain a hearing from pagans; but there is no suggestion that the Athenians' acknowledged ignorance of the divine nature was venial. [3]

'Established Christians' may well devote time to discussing this question. They can assure themselves that God takes people's spiritual opportunities into account. Luke, along with the other Synoptic Gospel writers, had recorded our Lord's own warning to those who had enjoyed the privilege of experiencing his earthly ministry , that at the judgment it will be more bearable for the people of Sodom, Tyre and Sidon than for them (Luke 10:12,14). Indeed our Lord went even further and claimed to know what the response of Tyre and Sidon would have been if they had seen his miracles – they would have repented (Luke 10:13). All this should help us to rest assured that God is able to act towards everyone with perfect justice, which was the conviction which Abraham held when faced with Sodom and Gomorrah: 'Will not the Judge of all the earth do right?' (Genesis 18:25).

How does Paul handle this question when in Athens and Lystra 'he is trying to gain a hearing from pagans'? What does he mean by his statement that God 'overlooked such ignorance' and that 'in his forbearance he had left the sins committed beforehand unpunished' (Romans 3:25b). In view of the teaching of the rest of Scripture, such as Romans 1-2, Paul cannot mean that the sins and ignorance of pagans is excusable. Again we turn to F. F. Bruce for help:

> In all these places it is implied that the coming of Christ means a fresh start. In the present place it is suggested that God has overlooked men's earlier ignorance of himself in view of the perfect revelation that has been given in the advent and work of Christ. [4]

In whatever way we may understand the attitude of God to sins and unbelief resulting from ignorance of the gospel, once Jesus has come and has made God known to men, there is no excuse for ignorance, and so God calls for repentance. The problem that ought really to concern unbelievers who raise this question, is not that of those who have never heard the gospel, but those who *have* heard it, and what they intend to do about it. This is especially the position of those who live in countries with a long Christian tradition, where there still is every opportunity to hear the gospel. And if they choose to ignore it, there is no doubt about their standing before the One by whom they will finally be judged. They will be without any excuse. If unbelievers are worried about whether those who have never heard will receive fair treatment, we can relieve them of such responsibility. After all it is hypothetical for believers and unbelievers alike. None of us will be called upon to judge the world. Judgment will be 'by the man he has appointed' (verse 31) and we can safely leave it to him.

In the light of that final judgment Paul calls upon his hearers to repent. God always demands this of those who have heard the gospel. It means basically a change of mind and outlook. It involves admitting that we have been wrong. More obviously we apply this to our moral failings, and no doubt there was plenty of scope for repentance in that sense in Athens, as for all of us. But what is called for here goes far deeper than the external wrongs of sinful lives. It concerns our entire relationship with God and our failure to give him his rightful place in our lives.

In the case of the Gentiles of New Testament times, one of the greatest hindrances in the way of a right relationship to God was idolatry. This was the ignorance of which they were called on to repent (verse 30). It was how Paul described the conversion of the Thessalonians when he recalled how they 'turned to God from idols to serve the living and true God' (1 Thessalonians 1:9).

Idolatry is an example of the presuppositions that can underlie the unbelief which so often stands in the way of a person coming to an understanding of the gospel. He holds on to his preconceived notions tenaciously, and ignores any ideas which do not agree with them. So if a person is to come to a knowledge of the truth, a hurdle he has to get over is to face the possibility that some of his cherished speculations might be wrong. This can be hard for some people, but it is a barrier in the way of finding God. So errors in understanding are matters for repentance, as the young minister, Timothy, had to recognise when Paul advised him that, 'Those who oppose him he must gently instruct, in the hope that God will grant them repentance leading them to a knowledge of the truth (2 Timothy 2:25).

One of the subtle and often unconscious ways that people hold on to their preconceived notions, and at the same time retain a respect for the preacher of the gospel, is to adapt what he says so that it fits in with their assumptions. After such mental editing, what people hear can be far removed from what we actually say. There were examples of this both in Athens and at Lystra. It was virtually what some of the Athenians did when they assumed that 'Jesus and the resurrection' were two extra deities to add to their collection. In Lystra it was worse. There they combined their polytheistic ideas with their admiration for Paul and Barnabas by treating them as gods! There, as in Athens, Paul called for repentance of such ignorance:

> Men, why are you doing this? We too are only men, human like you. We are bringing you good news, telling you to turn from these worthless things to the living God ... (Acts 14:15).

In Athens too, Paul realised that before his hearers could find the personal God revealed by Jesus, they must first repent of their idolatry, pantheistic ideas or whatever other misconceptions stood in the way of their acceptance of the true God.

The language with which Paul pressed this upon them is expressive. He was not engaging in a discussion, nor was he making a proposition which they may accept or decline as they pleased. Rather he was issuing a command from God: 'Now he commands all people everywhere to repent.' And the only alternative to submission is outright disobedience. This is why the word 'repent' on the lips of Old Testament prophets, John the Baptist, New Testament apostles and our Lord himself, is nearly always in the imperative. Once men and women have been exposed to the truths of the gospel, they are commanded to repent. Nor are they at liberty to postpone their response to suit their convenience, because it is '*now* he commands all people everywhere to repent'.

Here is the ultimate issue to be faced at the final judgment by those who have had the opportunity to respond to the gospel. Those who will be eternally punished will not just be 'those who do not know God', but those who 'do not *obey* the gospel of our Lord Jesus' (2 Thessalonians 1:8). And with the final judgment Paul concludes his Areopagus address.

11

THE FINAL JUDGMENT

Among the important facts of life revealed through 'Jesus and the resurrection' is human destiny, and with this Paul concludes his address to the Areopagus Council. Here is yet another question which has occupied the minds, not only of the ancient Greeks, but of human beings throughout history. There are, in fact, two closely related questions. With the inevitability of death no one can avoid asking what lies beyond the grave. But there are also questions about the future of human history – will it go on for ever or will it end one day? How we answer these questions is sure to have some effect on the way we live. It is the prospect that one day our lives will end that can give them some meaning and purpose. In this respect our lives are like a football match. If they went on for ever they would be meaningless. It is the anticipation that a final whistle will be blown that gives them meaning. So it is not surprising that Paul has something to say about human destiny.

Here is another realm in which Christian truth is at complete variance with popular speculations. There are many today who, like the Epicureans of Athens, expect nothing beyond the grave but oblivion and that is what they mean by being 'at rest'. Others have a vague expectation of life after death. It is often no more than being reunited to one's loved ones, and herein lies the only source of comfort in bereavement. 'She's gone to be with father' seems the nicest way to refer to a mother's death.

A very noticeable feature of present-day attitudes, as many writers have readily pointed out, is the reticence with which some people refer to death at all. During this century it has gradually replaced sex as the forbidden topic for polite conversation, and if it must be referred to, there are various euphemisms in use. Bereaved people often find themselves avoided by friends and neighbours, not because of any callousness on their part, but because they cannot cope with the reality of death.

Human speculation about life after death has covered a wide variety of possibilities. Some have regarded it as an extension of this present life, which would account for the earthly comforts and luxuries found in ancient Egyptian tombs. Others anticipate a return to this world by reincarnation. In the century of the New Testament there seems to have been an obsession with the fear of death. The foreboding with which it was regarded is evidenced by the epitaphs on pagan tombs of those days, which are in marked contrast to the expressions of confidence and hope on the graves of early Christians. The Epicurean answer was to destroy both fears and hopes by their denial of any existence beyond the grave. For the Stoics, on the other hand, death was another harsh reality before which to display the stiff upper lip.

Then what about the future prospects for the world? A popular view in Paul's day was the cyclic theory, with ages following each other in cycles. Each age was expected to end in destruction, with a subsequent rebirth to usher in the next. Another widely held view has been the expectation of an approaching Utopia. This was in vogue at the beginning of the twentieth century, which was hailed as the golden age towards which the human race had been evolving during its entire history, and in which all its problems would be left behind by the march of scientific progress. J. A. Symons expressed it thus in the opening verse of a poem:

> These things shall be: a loftier race
> Than e'er the world hath known shall rise
> With flame of freedom in their souls
> And light of knowledge in their eyes.

The rest of the poem continued with expectations that man would 'spill no drop of blood', would 'plant man's lordship firm', and 'man shall love man, with heart as pure ...' finishing with the assertion that 'every life shall be a song, when all the earth is paradise.' Exactly halfway through this century, on the first day of January, 1950, Dr Martyn Lloyd-Jones, from the pulpit of Westminster Chapel in London, made this assertion:

> Standing as we do halfway through this century, are we not compelled to say that no century has so disappointed the prophets, and has so falsified the confident optimistic predictions.

And now the second half of this century has almost passed. Could anyone contradict this assessment? What are the expectations for the next century? The apostles of secular optimism, if there are any left, are understandably silent.

Now for Paul, whatever may be the changing fortunes which the world will experience in the meantime, the ultimate future event with which we must reckon is the Day of Judgment, and with this disturbing fact he reached the conclusion of his address:

> He has set a day when he will judge the world with justice by the man he has appointed. He has given proof of this to all men by raising him from the dead (Acts 17:31).

It was by no means unusual for Paul to associate the coming judgment with 'a day', a term which originated in the Old Testament. The prophet Amos spoke of the 'Day of the Lord' which was to be one in which God's honour would be openly vindicated. No longer would ungodly men be able to oppose his will and blaspheme his name with impunity. It would be a day in which men would be judged and punished for their sins and, as Amos was at pains to point out, this would include Israel as well as the surrounding pagan tribes (Amos 5:18).

In the New Testament this term is taken over and applied to the Second Coming of Jesus. There are also variations such as 'the day of Christ', 'the day of God's wrath' or simply 'that day'.[1] In the meantime the world is having its own day. This was how

Jesus viewed the time of his arrest: 'This is your hour – when darkness reigns' (Luke 22:53). But God's day is coming when, in the language of Isaiah, 'the LORD alone will be exalted in that day' (Isaiah 2:11).

Furthermore Paul declares that God 'has *set* a day'. Our final destiny will not be a random affair thrown up by chance. Nor will it arise from the out-working of automatic, impersonal rules. Instead it will be determined by the deliberate, intelligent plan of a personal God who works according to a care-fully arranged programme. So there are what the Bible calls 'times and dates' (Acts 1:7; 1 Thessalonians 5:1) as the world's history moves on towards its God-appointed climax.

As in the Old Testament, the day to which Paul was looking forward will be one of judgment in which God who has exercised his providential rule over the earth, will intervene as Judge. Because we have been created as moral beings, we shall have to render ac-count of our lives. This is all part of being God's offspring, created in his image. We are not helpless robots with our behaviour determined solely by our endocrine glands. We can say that in punishing us God pays us a compliment. He is treating us as responsi-ble human beings, who are answerable to him for the way we have lived the lives he has given us.

Then there is another feature which Paul picks out for mention. God's judgment will be exercised 'with justice' or 'in righteousness' to use the alter-native translation of this frequently occurring Bible word. In the Septuagint version of the Psalms it describes the principles by which God exercises judgment. [2] There is a vast difference between this and the ideas that many in Paul's audience would have had about the dealings of the gods with men. Their gods and goddesses were anything but righteous in their deeds. The God of the Jews and Christians, on the other hand, had shown himself as one who always acts righteously, especially when he rules and arbitrates over human affairs, whether in salvation or in judgment. It shows that God is not like a benevolent grandfather who, because he has no ultimate responsibility for his grandchildren, can afford to turn a blind eye to their misdemeanours, and so gain an immediate popularity with them but eventually lose their respect. Nor would we expect a human judge to behave in that way and allow his feelings to affect his judgments. We can hardly expect anything less of a holy God who 'is righteous in all his ways' (Psalm 145:17).

There is great comfort to be derived from these facts about God, and from the realisation that the universe is ruled by one who is uncompromisingly righteous. It is also reassuring when we contemplate such a God judging men. The perfect justice of God also covers the problem of those who, because of mental illness, can claim diminished responsibility for their actions. We have already referred to Abraham who, when concerned for any righteous people that might be living in Sodom when God punished that city, took refuge in this great truth when he exclaimed, 'Will not the Judge of all the earth do right?'

(Genesis 18:25). We can do the same.

Although we may not be too sure of what to make of Paul's point about God overlooking the times of ignorance, we can be quite sure that however God tackles this problem it will be perfectly just. At the same time there is a sobering thought. The position of those who, like the Athenians after the visit of Paul, are no longer in ignorance, is left in no doubt. They are among those who are now 'commanded to repent' (Acts 17:30), so they are without excuse. Let us look again at the point Jesus made to the people who heard him speak and saw his works:

> Woe to you, Korazin! Woe to you, Bethsaida! For if the miracles that were performed in you had been performed in Tyre and Sidon, they would have repented long ago, sitting in sackcloth and ashes (Luke 10:13).

Taking this on its own it could appear that there was something unfair in the way that Tyre and Sidon had been treated. But having shown a knowledge of how they would have repented given sufficient opportunity, Jesus continues: 'But it will be more tolerable for Tyre and Sidon at the judgment than for you.'

Translated into modern terms this might read: 'It shall be more tolerable in the judgment for ignorant head-hunters who have never heard the gospel, than for those in Western countries who have had the Bible in their own language for centuries, and are within walking distance of a church where the gospel of Christ is preached and yet prefer to ignore him for lives dominated by material pleasure.' Here is a disquieting difference between pre-Christian and post-Christian paganism, between those who have had no opportunity to hear the gospel and those who have had every opportunity.

God's dealing with man and his wrong-doing can be likened to a phrase of music, especially a more traditional hymn tune consisting of a series of chords. If you stop playing before the end it can be quite unsatisfying and even discordant. But if you play to the end the final chord will resolve it. [3] At present, because of sin in the world, there are many injustices to be put right and many wrongs that cry out to be punished. The people of God have often been bothered by this and how the name of God can be blasphemed with impunity. There are examples in the Psalms of men calling upon God to vindicate his honour by bringing wrongdoers to account.[4] And this is the very thing that God will do when he intervenes again to 'judge the world with justice'.

This judgment will be exercised 'by the man he has appointed'. From the reference to the resurrection that follows, it is clear that 'the man' is Jesus Christ who is the one by whom God will judge the world. One naturally wonders whether Paul had in mind the 'one like a son of man' of Daniel's vision (Daniel 7:13). That was the scripture Jesus quoted at his trial when being questioned by the High Priest about his divine claims and which led to a charge of blasphemy (Mark 14:61-64). There the Messiah is seen sharing God's glory and authority, and mediating his judgment. So the final judgment will be both

'God's judgment' (Romans 14:10) and 'the judgment seat of Christ' (2 Corinthians 5:10) for, as Jesus claimed, God 'has given him authority to judge because he is the Son of Man' (John 5:27). The message of Amos to Old Testament Israel was 'Prepare to meet your God' (Amos 2:14). Since the resurrection of Christ God's message to the world is 'Prepare to meet the risen Christ'.

There is something very striking about this reference, on the lips both of Jesus and Paul, to Jesus in judgment as 'the man'. Before the judgment seat men will be confronted by the Man! The standard will be not only what God intended us to be when he created us and from which we have fallen short, but what he has demonstrated in the incarnate life of Jesus. That is what it really means to be 'God's offspring' created in his image. Thus there will be no enforcement of some arbitrary or alien standard, but only the law of true human nature. The accusation will be that of failing to be truly human.

How can we be ready to face that day with confidence? It is by seeking him as God has intended we should, by repenting of our man-made ideas of him and by submitting ourselves to all that Jesus has made known of him. But how can we be sure that history will reach its climax in the final judgment? The answer is simple: 'He has given proof of this to all men by raising him from the dead' (Acts 17:31b).

So we are back to where we started – 'Jesus and the resurrection'. It was to explain the significance of this that Paul had been first brought before the

Athenian council. He ends by returning to it and stating, as he does elsewhere, that if proof is wanted that Jesus really will come again in judgment, it will be found in the evidence of his resurrection (1 Corinthians 15:20; 1 Thessalonians 1:10; 4:14). So the question whether the Easter story is historical fact is not of mere academic interest. If it is true we are bound to take seriously both the promises and warnings of Jesus. This is the crucial nature of what Paul was speaking about in Athens when they asked him, 'May we know what this new teaching is that you are presenting?'

12

RESULTS

The result of Paul's address to the Areopagus and his time in Athens are not what many evangelists of today would exactly welcome: 'A few men became followers of Paul and believed' (Acts 17:34). But there was also a negative reaction which Luke mentions first:

> When they heard about the resurrection of the dead, some of them sneered, but others said, 'We want to hear you again on this subject' (Acts 17:32).

It has been suggested that it was the Epicureans who laughed at the resurrection, while the more thoughtful and polite Stoics were willing to hear Paul again. But it is not only Epicureans who dismiss the resurrection out of hand. Among the Greeks there was a widely held belief in the immortality of the soul, but they excluded any idea of a bodily resurrection. They may well have recalled the words that Aeschyllus had put into the mouth of the god Apollo: 'Once a man dies and the earth drinks up his blood, there is no resurrection.' As F. F. Bruce has noticed, these sentiments were 'expressed on the occasion when the very court of the Areopagus was founded by the city's patron goddess Athene'. [1]

A bodily resurrection is also alien to much popular thought today. It is noticeable that when it is discussed by those who dismiss it, the historical evidence is rarely faced. Was Luke, for example, a capable historian, who had reliable sources which he could handle with competence? Many scholars would answer such questions in the affirmative. Were the apostles reliable witnesses of the resurrection? Or were they all mistaken or willing to die a martyr's death for what they knew to be untrue? So many, however, as we pointed out in Chapter 5, base their objections simply on their refusal to accept the possibility of God intervening supernaturally in the world's history, and this closes their minds to any historical evidence there may be. But just because we don't encounter supernatural interventions by God on a par with what happened in the first century in our experience today, that does not mean that God never has worked in that way. Such miraculous interventions by God have always been exceptional. They were unusual in the Old Testament, being restricted to the Exodus, the time of Elijah and Elisha and the Babylonian exile. Chad Walsh suggested that such prejudices are

> as though a race of short-lived midges, breeding dozens of generations in one summer, were to assume that trees always have leaves and that leaves are always green. [2]

One feels entitled to ask whether those who have prided themselves with the description 'free-thinkers' have minds which are quite as free as they assume, for when it comes to facing the possibility of God intervening supernaturally, their minds are anything but free.

There were others among Paul's audience, however, who were more promising. They were prepared to respond with the willingness to 'hear you again on this subject'. What subsequently happened to them we are not told. Also we don't know how sincere all of them were. Howard Marshall thinks that 'the contrast expressed with the first group may suggest that this was a more positive reaction'. [3] J. S. Stewart became convinced that they were true seekers through hearing Paul:

> I used to think this was just polite evasion, the eternal refuge of the procrastinating spirit. I am not so sure of it now. I think they were genuinely touched and moved by the dramatic *kerygma*. [4]

Anyway, what we do know is that Paul was prepared to conduct regular discussions over a period of two years 'in the lecture hall of Tyrannus' at Ephesus (Acts 19:9). This must always be provided for in evangelism. Not every convert is prepared to make a commitment at the first hearing of the gospel, especially those with no Christian background. But genuine seekers will be willing to make use of further opportunities to consider the claims of Christ. Indeed, those who readily make response, may just as readily fall away. The Parable of the Sower makes this point eloquently. Those who readily 'receive the

word with joy' are like rocky ground where the seed
springs up quickly. But they 'have no root' because
they are shallow like the thin layer of soil on rocky
ground. And so for the same reason they fall away as
soon as the pressures of the world make Christian
commitment difficult. I well remember undertaking
a survey of those who had professed conversion under my own ministry in a London church. I discovered that a far higher proportion of those who had
attended a series of classes before making a commitment survived as Christians than those who readily signed a decision card at the first hearing of the
gospel. Those engaged in evangelistic work among
young people, and find it easy to extract professions
of conversion from teenagers, ought to think care-
fully about this.

Nevertheless there were those who 'became followers of Paul and believed'. I assume that this was
the result of Paul's entire ministry in Athens including his time in the market place, because Luke distinguishes Dionysius from the others as 'a member
of the Areopagus'. Another convert Luke mentions
is 'a woman named Damaris'. Nothing is known of
her, but we assume she must have been a lady of
some distinction for Luke to mention her by name.
Ramsay suggests that she may have been an educated
foreign woman 'in view of the unlikelihood of an
ordinary Athenian woman being present at any public meeting addressed by Paul'. [5] Another possibility
mentioned by Bruce is that she was a God-fearer who
heard him in the synagogue.

How do we number the converts? Whether we compare them with the results Peter had seen under very different circumstances in Jerusalem, or with the entire population of Athens, they were no more than what Luke calls 'a few'. At the same time he is prepared in the same verse to speak of 'a number of others'.

What is important is that Paul's ministry in Athens led to the planting of a church there. His aim was not only to see the salvation of individuals, but to plant churches, and with his eye for missionary strategy, to do this in a centre as important as Athens would more than compensate for the small number of converts. It may have taken a little time to get organised before Paul could confidently claim that a church had been founded there. Perhaps this would account for there being no known 'Epistle to the Athenians'. This also may be why he seems to have regarded Corinth as the first church in Achaia. We conclude this from the way he describes 'the house of Stephanas' as 'the firstfruits of Achaia' (1 Corinthians 16:15, KJV). [6] A possible guess is that a church could be formed more easily in Corinth, with the house of Stephanas as a suitable meeting place.

We do know, however, that a church was established in Athens, although we know little of its earlier history. During the first century, there is some evidence that Dionysius became the first of a line of bishops. This is quite likely because the first converts often became church leaders. From the small beginnings which resulted from Paul's visit, the church sooner or later grew, because by the first half of the second century it was quite flourishing. One of its major contributions was in the apologists it produced, the best known of whom was Athenagorus, a second-century Athenian, who wrote *A Plea for the Christians* and *On the Resurrection*. In view of Paul's emphasis on the resurrection, the latter title naturally attracts our attention. Its author was converted through reading the Scriptures with the original intention to discredit them and, significantly enough, it was the resurrection which convinced him. Apologists like him followed in the steps of the apostle in presenting the faith meaningfully to the thinking people of their day.

13

CONCLUSION

Before concluding our study of Paul's time in Athens, we ought to give some consideration to the theory I referred to in the preface which, if it were true, would seriously undermine much of the value of the Areopagus address. It is the suggestion that Paul was adapting his views of God to the thinking of the Athenians, especially that of the Stoics, by quoting their literature. He has even been given the distinction by those who approve of this type of approach, of anticipating such twentieth-century names as Bultmann, Tillich and John Robinson! Some have maintained that, except for the conclusion, the address is Hellenistic rather than Christian, and have decided therefore that it was not even Pauline, but composed by Luke or someone else. This highly critical theory has been effectively answered by a Swedish scholar, Bertil Gartner. To save space, here is John Stott's useful summary of his main points:

> His thesis was (i) that the background to the speech is to be found rather in Hebrew than in Greek thought, and especially in the Old Testament; (ii) that it has parallels in the apologetic preaching of Hellenistic Judaism; and (iii) that it is genuinely Pauline in the sense that its main features reflect Paul's thought in

his letters .... So it is not difficult to affirm with a good conscience that the voice we hear in the Areopagus address is the voice of the authentic Paul. [1]

At the same time there are those who are quite prepared to accept that the speech is Pauline, but claim that it was inadequate, which was the reason for the meagre results, and that Paul himself later realised his mistake. Much has been made, for evidence of this, of Paul's assertion about his preaching in Corinth, whither he proceeded immediately after leaving Athens:

> When I came to you, brothers, I did not come with eloquence or superior wisdom as I proclaimed to you the testimony about God. For I resolved to know nothing while I was with you except Jesus Christ and him crucified (1 Corinthians 2:2).

It has been said that Paul was contrasting his emphasis in Corinth from the line he had taken in Athens, the implication being that he was now deprecating what he now regarded as 'eloquence or superior wisdom' in his Areopagus address, and its lack of emphasis on 'Jesus Christ and him crucified'.

Firstly, *what about the suggestion that Paul was admitting that he had pandered to the intellectual climate of Athens?* How can it be asserted, as some have done, that Paul was accommodating his teaching to the pantheistic views of the Stoics, in face of his declaration of the transcendence of God? Having, in loyalty to Old Testament teaching, set him forth as in no way dependent on his creatures, Paul

surely said all he needed to prevent any misunderstanding that in quoting Greek writers he was ap-
proving of all their views. No doubt Paul could have
made a strong appeal to them had he described God,
to use the pantheistic language of modern writers
like John Robinson, as 'the ground of our being'.
Indeed if he were trying to ingratiate himself with
the sophisticated Athenians, and demonstrate to them
how intellectually respectable and cultured a Christian preacher can be, he could hardly have made a
worse blunder than to tell them that God commanded
them to repent, and to base this on a warning of judgment to come!

And just because he quoted Greek writers is no
ground for assuming he wanted them to think he
shared their views. F. F. Bruce compares this with
the way that preachers often quote Tennyson's saying that 'More things are wrought by prayer than this
world dreams of':

> A Christian preacher today may quote the well-known
> lines about prayer from Tennyson's *Morte d'Arthur*
> without subscribing either to the ideals of the Arthurian
> legend or to Tennyson's religious position. [2]

*What of the suggestion that Paul himself had later
misgivings about his method in Athens?* There is no
indication that Luke, who was a close associate of
Paul, was aware of this. Nor is there the slightest
hint that Luke was presenting Paul's speech on Mars
Hill as a mistake to be avoided. Nor do Luke or Paul
(or any other biblical writers for that matter) ever

regard a small number of converts as a sign of failure, or a criterion as to 'the correctness of the message'. [3] Nor does Paul give us any ground for imagining that behind what he wrote to the Corinthians was his experience in Athens. In that epistle his mind is completely taken up with his readers and their problems and, as John Stott has rightly affirmed, his message and method when he first preached there were 'because of the anticipated challenges of proud Corinth, not because of his supposed failure in Athens'. [4]

Next we face the allegation that Paul neglected the atonement in Athens. There is no proof of this. To begin with Luke does not claim to give an exhaustive account, but rather picks out the distinctive points of Paul's ministry there. These were that when Paul was faced with an audience who did not share any of his presuppositions, he based his arguments on the person of Christ and the evidence for the resurrection. There is no reason to suppose that 'in the market-place day by day' Paul did not also speak about the death of Christ and, from what we know of Paul, it is virtually certain that he did.

As for the Areopagus address itself, as we have already pointed out, this was primarily to explain the significance of 'Jesus and the Resurrection'. He was able to show how this leads to a knowledge of God and an understanding of the nature of man – necessary to a proper appreciation of the gospel. But we must also agree with John Stott when he asks:

How could he proclaim the resurrection without mentioning the death which preceded it? And how could he call for repentance without mentioning the faith in Christ which always accompanies it? [5]

It may be that Paul intended to speak of the death of Christ after his reference to the final judgment, but that the sneering which greeted his mention of the resurrection brought his speech to a premature end. Some, however, were impressed by what Paul had said and wanted to hear further from him. Is it not likely that, having declared their willingness to repent of their errors, they were further instructed in other gospel truths, including the meaning of Christ's death, at some kind of 'after-meeting' before they 'became followers of Paul and believed'?

Let C. K. Barrett summarise the conclusions we have drawn about Luke's account in Acts and Paul's claim to the Corinthians:

We may be confident that Luke did not intend to describe a lapse on the part of his hero, and there is nothing in Paul's own words to the Corinthians to suggest a change of plan; rather he intends to describe his normal practice, though this normal practice was bound to appear the more striking in such a place as Corinth. He is not contrasting his evangelistic method he employed in Corinth with that which he employed elsewhere, but with that which others employed in Corinth (*Moffatt*). [6]

*   *   *   *

How do we apply what we have learnt? To answer it would really demand another book with an analysis of the contemporary scene, for which I have neither the space nor the competence to undertake. Perhaps someone else with sufficient expertise would do so. In the meantime I will simply pick out some of the issues which seem to me to call for further discussion. I will group them under three headings: the men, the methods and the message.

By men I mean both men and women engaged in evangelism. To begin with there must be strong motivation. That is the first thing we are told about Paul when he surveyed the scene on arrival in Athens: 'He was greatly distressed'. What he saw impressed on him the lost condition of the Athenians in spite of all their learning. But it was not only concern for the spiritual needs of his fellow humans which moved him. He was jealous for the honour of God when he saw the profanity of their idolatry. Unless we to some extent share such concern, the study we have undertaken will never be more than academic.

Whereas every Christian has a duty to grasp every opportunity to witness by life and lip, the New Testament recognises that some have the gift of evangelism, and that this is a deliberate part of God's ordering of leadership in his church. What we need to face, however, is that the type of ministry represented by the term 'evangelist' in the New Testament is not necessarily someone who addresses religious meetings which other Christians have organised for him. There is a place for that and Paul's preaching in the synagogues is a perfect New Testament example. But if we are to face the desperate needs of the pagan world, the evangelist will need the gift for the spade-work of making the initial contact with unbelievers. Instead of conducting a series of meetings over a week or two and then moving on, he will probably find the need to stay longer in the same district. We are not told how long Paul remained in Athens, but in Corinth he spent eighteen months (Acts 18:11) and in Ephesus he stayed for two years (Acts 19:10). According to 1 Corinthians 16:9 the reason for his prolonged stay in Ephesus was 'because a great door for effective work has opened to me'. We assume he had no other missions booked in his diary! This will involve working alongside local Christians, that is supposing, unlike first century Athens, there are any!

When we come to method, we have to ask our-selves how tied we are to approaches which assume a Christian background. We have seen the need to go to where people are in the example of Paul in the market place. We also need to do this in the language we employ. This can be especially difficult for those who have been Christians for some time, including those brought up in the faith as children. Here a new convert, in spite of his lack of knowledge of many aspects of Christian teaching, is often at an advan-tage, before he has learnt 'the language of Zion' and is still able to express himself in terms which the ordinary person can understand. Here Paul again is an example. In spite of having been steeped in rab-binical language and thought forms through his background as a Pharisee, as the apostle to the Gentiles he took the trouble to master their language and the way they thought. Although the Areopagus address is full of Old Testament truths, Paul's language was essentially Athenian, even including quotations from their literature to illustrate his points. We could say that he was like Moses whose effectiveness as a leader of Israel was greatly enhanced by being 'educated in all the wisdom of the Egyptians' (Acts 7:22). We can apply this to the importance of secular reading as one way of educating ourselves.

Effective communication, however, is not only a matter of language. What we say must be seen to be relevant to people's real needs. This is precisely what Paul did when he made their idolatry his starting point. And he did not simply refer to the futility of idolatry in general, which many of his hearers may well have been ready to admit, but with a stroke of genius he picked on the altar to the unknown god. The irony of it! With their vast heritage of human learning, the institutions they possessed and the celebrated names among their leading thinkers, they still have an altar to an unknown god! And here was where the gospel came into its own: 'What therefore you worship as unknown, this I proclaim to you!'

Surely today is full of parallels. We are vastly more privileged than the ancient Athenians. Instead of the speculations of their philosophers we enjoy the concrete results of science and technology. People can fill their homes with all the luxuries that money can buy, but those same homes can break up because they are unable to maintain stable relationships with each other. Vast sums are spent on tranquillisers every year – hardly the sign of a healthy society. In spite of widespread education and rapidly increasing knowledge, many of those who are willing to interrupt their quest for material luxury and entertainment to stop and think about life, are having to admit that it lacks any meaning and purpose. This is the logical outcome of an agnosticism which knows no god, and a materialism which views human beings as nothing more than highly developed biological machines. How could the gospel be anything but relevant to such a society!

Our language and the way we apply the message will vary according to the people we are speaking to. If the conceptual language of our hearers is the strip cartoon, then we have to adapt ourselves accordingly. Paul showed the same flexibility. We have made references to Paul's time at Lystra (Acts 14:8-18). As in Athens the issue there was idolatry and so Paul declared to them also the living and personal God of Christian revelation. But in contrast they were an uneducated and agricultural community, and so Paul singled out God's providential control over nature which would have been of particular concern to them.

Now, although Paul's example encourages us to adapt our style to those we are out to reach, when it comes to the actual message we must be clear and uncompromising even if, as Paul found in Athens, it means derision on the part of some. Yet it is always tempting, out of a genuine desire to commend our message to unbelieving minds, to play down any aspect of the truth which might make it unpopular. The New Testament churches were not lacking in those who had succumbed to this temptation. In Galatia the Judaizers wanted to modify the vital doctrine of justification by faith to accommodate the prejudices of those with a Jewish background. At Colossae there were others who found a way to adapt the doctrine of Christ's person to suit the presuppositions of Greek philosophy. Paul had every opportunity to feel the same pressures from sophisticated Greeks who subjected the doctrines both of the cross and resurrection to ridicule.

The pages of church history are full of examples of attempts to bridge the gulf between biblical truth and secular thought by sacrificing vital aspects of Christian truth. J. I Packer has sketched out some typical examples:

> In the second century, Gnosticism aspired to remodel the doctrine of salvation in the light of an oriental dualism which taught that matter as such was evil; salvation, therefore, it was held, should be conceived as deliverance from the body and the material world. In the fourth century, Arianism aspired to remodel the Church's Christology by the light of Greek philosophical ideas about God, which made it impossible to think of Jesus Christ as divine. In the eighteenth century, the Deists wished to remodel the doctrine of providence in the light of the then-popular view of the universe as a self-contained machine, and to make men think of God as an absentee landlord, who had left the world to run itself. The nineteenth-century liberals tried to remodel the doctrine of human nature and grace in

the light of the theory of evolution, maintaining that sin was just a transitional stage in the steady march of mankind under Christ's leadership, towards inevitable perfection. [7]

And twentieth-century theological liberals are still at it. This time it is the attempt to commend Christianity to a materialistic society that discounts the supernatural, by keeping quiet about the miracles of Jesus, his virgin conception and bodily resurrection or, if challenged about them, by explaining them away. Many years ago I heard Cardinal Heenan on the radio observe that some exponents defend Christianity by seeing that there is nothing left to defend!

We are sometimes told that we are to answer the questions people ask. But what if, in their blindness, they ask the wrong questions? Some make their acceptance of the Christian faith depend on whether we can give a satisfactory explanation to problems which any fool can raise and which no human being in this life can answer – chestnuts like the problems of suffering, the origin of evil and so on. Some imagine that they can justify their unbelief by pointing at the inconsistencies of some Christians. During this present life, before sin and temptation are finally eradicated, from the New Testament onwards there have admittedly been professing Christians who have let the side down. Others base their discussions about Christianity on their subjective speculations about the supernatural. Now all these are questions to be faced sooner or later, and Christians find that the Bible throws light on them all, even though we are not always told all we would like to know. They are, however, not the basic questions on which the truth of Christianity depends and with which Paul challenged the Athenians: Who was Jesus, were his divine claims true, and did he really rise again from death? Is the apostolic witness to him authentic, or did they, for reasons best known to themselves, make it all up? These were the questions which Paul, who assumed that it is God who sets the agenda, pressed on his hearers in the market place.

Although nearly two thousand years have passed since Paul stood on Mars Hill, multitudes are still in a state of agnosticism with nothing more than an 'unknown god' to provide some meaning to life. Chance or fate are still the only alternatives to the personal God who can be found by faith in Christ and the only way to account for life with all its problems and sufferings. Then what about the doctrine of man? Humanistic views on offer today are a poor substitute for the dignified view that follows from a biblical understanding of man's creation. And where will it all end as end it must? We don't need a Bible to tell us that everyone must some day face death and what lies beyond. How humbly, honestly and responsibly everyone should consider the claims of Jesus Christ because, if they are true, he is the one to whom they will have to render account and he is no unknown god!

Notes

Chapter 1: Sowing or Reaping

1. e.g. Acts 18:9-10; 2 Corinthians 4:7-12.
2. *Archbishops' Committee of Inquiry on the Evangelistic Work of the Church* (1918).
3. Francis Schaeffer: *Death in the City* (Inter-Varsity Press, 1969) p.12.
4. Michael Green: *Evangelism in the Early Church* (Hodder and Stoughton, 1970) p.28.
5. *On the Other Side - The Report of the Evangelical Alliance's Commission on Evangelism* (Scripture Union, 1968) p.173.

Chapter 2: Art Forms and Idols

1. E. M. Blaiklock: *The Areopagus Address,* Rendle Short Memorial Lecture, 1964, p.2.
2. e.g. 1 Kings 23:43; 2 Kings 14:4; 15:4.
3. Michael Green: *Evangelism in the Early Church* (Hodder and Stoughton, 1970), p.127.
4. John Eddison: *Christian Standards* (Scripture Union, 1965), p.17.
5. R. W. Dale: *The Ten Commandments* (Hodder and Stoughton, 1871), p.43.
6. C. K. Barrett: *The Epistle to the Romans* (A & C. Black, 1957), p.39.
7. *Ibid.*, p.3.

Chapter 3: In the Market Place

1. John R. W. Stott: *The Message of Acts* (Inter-Varsity Press, 1990), p.281.
2. R. C. Lucas: *Fullness and Freedom* (Inter-Varsity Press, 1980) p.173-174.
3. *Ibid.*, p.281.
4. J. I. Packer: *'Fundamentalism' and the Word of God* (Inter-Varsity Fellowship, 1958), p.135.

Chapter 4: Chance or Fate?

1. Francis Schaeffer: *Escape from Reason* (Inter-Varsity Fellowship, 1968), p.7.

2. Michael Green: *Man Alive* (Inter-Varsity Fellowship, 1967), p.5,10.

3. We may note in passing that science too, especially when coupled with materialistic presuppositions, has its own version of these two points of view. On the one hand there is determinism, which views the material universe as a closed system, in which everything which happens is predetermined by previous events which ultimately consist in the movements of atoms and molecules. Human behaviour is just part of it, and this is caused by nothing other than electrical impulses in the brain, and chemical secretions of the glands. The idea of any person possessing free will is a delusion.

Science also sees chance as the alternative ultimate arbiter of events. Democritus, the propounder of atomic theory in the ancient world, one of whose pupils, incidentally, taught Epicurus in his earlier years, maintained that all that happens is caused by the random movements of atomic particles. When these ancient atomic theories were revived in the seventeenth century, the element of chance was superseded by the idea of a clockwork universe, controlled predictably by fixed laws. More recently, however, the view that chance is the ultimate cause was revived in 1927 by the Heisenberg uncertainty principle, which sees the fortuitous movements and collisions of atomic particles as the deciding factor.

4. F. F. Bruce: *The Book of Acts* (Marshall, Morgan and Scott, 1962), p.351.

Chapter 5: Jesus and the Resurrection

1. e.g. Acts 2:32; 3:15; 5:32; 10:39-41.

2. Michael Green: *Evangelism in the Early Church* (Hodder and Stoughton, 1970), p.72.

3. R. Bultmann: *Kerygma and Myth* (S.P.C.K., 1962), p.42.

4. Lesslie Newbigin: *The Gospel in a Pluralist Society* (S.P.C.K., 1989), p.11.

5. Frank Morison: *Who moved the Stone?* (Faber and Faber, 1930).

6. Michael Green: *Runaway World* (Inter-Varsity Press, 1968), ch.1.

7. Many will be acquainted with *Basic Christianity* by John Stott, which has rightly enjoyed probably the largest and widest circulation of any evangelistic book this century. It is noteworthy that, after an opening chapter entitled, 'The Right Approach', the next three chapters are headed: The Claims of Christ; The Character of Christ; The Resurrection of Christ.

Chapter 6: What's new?

1. F. F. Bruce: *The Book of Acts* (Marshall, Morgan and Scott, 1962), p.355.

2. Christopher Booker: *The Neophiliacs* (Fontana, 1970), p.99.

3. *Ibid.*, p.95.

4. Kenneth Boulding, quoted by Alvin Toffler: *Future Shock* (Pan Books, 1970), p.22.

5. *Ibid.*, p.33.

Chapter 7: The Unknown God

1. F. F. Bruce: *The Book of Acts* (Marshall, Morgan and Scott, 1962), p.355.

2. Quoted by John Calvin: *The Institutes of the Christian Religion.*

3. Francis Schaeffer: *The God who is There* (Hodder and Stoughton, 1968), p.89.

4. N. B. Stonehouse: *Paul before the Areopagus* (Tyndale Press, 1957), p.19.

5. Malcolm A. Jeeves: *The Scientific Enterprise and the Christian Faith* (Tyndale Press, 1969), p.9.

6. The influence of the Reformation and the rejection of Aristotle on the rise of modern science is clearly shown by Herbert Butterfield: *The Origins of Modern Science* (G.Bell and Sons,1957).

7. *Ibid.*, p.12.

8. W. K. C. Guthrie: *Greek Philosophy* (Cambridge University Press, 1953), p.190.

9. *Ibid.*, p.24.

10. e.g. Acts 4:2; 17:3; 1 Corinthians 9:14; 11:26; Philippians 1:17-18; Colossians 1:27-28.

11. Cp 1 Corinthians 2:12 (cp 'to us' in the emphatic first place in the sentence).

12. A. M. Ramsay: *Introducing the Christian Faith* (S.C.M. Press, 1960), p.38.

13. Lesslie Newbigin: *The Gospel in a Pluralist Society* (S.P.C.K., 1989), p.4.

Chapter 8: The Personal God

1. Lesslie Newbigin: *Honest Religion for Secular Man* (S.C.M. Press, 1966), p.32.

2. C. S. Lewis: *Miracles* (Geoffrey Bles, 1947), p.99.

3. *op cit.*, p.39.

4. John R.W. Stott: *The Message of Acts* (Inter-Varsity Press, 1990), p.286.

5. Derek Kidner: *The Message of Jeremiah* (Inter-Varsity Press, 1987), p.92.

Chapter 9: God's Offspring

1. Robert Brow: *Religion - Origins and Ideas* (Tyndale Press, 1966), p.76.

2. Emil Brunner: *Man in Revolt*, translated by Olive Wyon (Lutterworth Press, 1939) p.82.

3. Arnold Lunn and Garth Lean: *The Cult of Softness* (Blandford Press, 1965), p.64.

4. *Ibid.*, p.44.

5. E. M. Blaiklock: *The Areopagus Address*, Rendle Short Memorial Lecture, 1964, p.7.

6. Derek Kidner: *Genesis* (Tyndale Press, 1967), p.50.

7. Emil Brunner: *Our Faith*, translated by John W.Rilling (S.C.M Press, 1949), p.37.

8. T. M. Kitwood: *What is Human?* (Inter-Varsity Press, 1970), p.95.

9. Emil Brunner: *Man in Revolt*, translated by Olive Wyon Lutterworth Press, 1939) p.102.

10. F. F. Bruce: *The Epistle of Paul to the Romans* (Tyndale Press, 1963) p.86f.

11. F. F. Bruce: *The Book of Acts* (Marshall, Morgan and Scott, 1962), p.361.

12. I am indebted to Lunn and Lean for these quotations. *Ibid.* p.62-63.

13. N. B. Stonehouse: *Paul before the Areopagus* (Tyndale Press, 1957), p.27.

Chapter 10: God's Demand

1. E. M. Blaiklock: *The Areopagus Address,* Rendle Short Memorial Lecture, 1964, p.15.

2. C. S. Lewis: *Miracles* (Geoffrey Bles, 1947), p.99.

3. F. F. Bruce: *The Book of Acts* (Marshall, Morgan and Scott, 1962), p.359.

4. *Ibid.*, p.361.

Chapter 11: The Final Judgment
1. e.g. Romans 2:5; Philippians 1:6,10; 1 Thessalonians 5:2,4.
2. e.g. Psalm 9:8; 96:13; 98:9.
3. For an example look at the tune *Moscow* and play the ninth chord from the end!
4. e.g. Psalm 10:15; 74:10-11; 79:6-7; 83; 139:19-20.

Chapter 12: Results
1. F. F. Bruce: *The Book of the Acts* (Marshall, Morgan and Scott, 1962), p.363-364.
2. Chad Walsh: *Stop Looking and Listen* (S.C.M Press Ltd, 1948), p.25.
3. I. Howard Marshall: *The Acts of the Apostles* (Inter-Varsity Press, 1980), p.291.
4. J. S. Stewart: *A Faith to Proclaim* (London, 1953), p.117.
5. I am indebted to F. F. Bruce for this reference to Sir William Ramsay: Ibid., p.364.
6. 'Firstfruits' (KJV) is a literal translation of *aparchia*. It is used both in classical Greek and in the Septuagint (e.g. Numbers 15:18-21) of first fruits (including animals) offered in sacrifice. It is difficult to sustain the rendering 'the first converts in Achaia' found in modern translations. This is surely a misleading interpretation when Acts 17 makes it quite clear that the first actual converts in Achaia were in Athens and not Corinth.

Chapter 13: Conclusion
1. John R. W. Stott: *The Message of Acts* (Inter-Varsity Press, 1990), p.288-289.
2. F. F. Bruce: *The Apostolic Defence of the Gospel* (Inter-Varsity Fellowship, 1959), p.37.
3. N. B. Stonehouse: *Paul before the Areopagus* (Tyndale Press) p.34

4. *Ibid.*, p.290.
5. *Ibid.*, p.289.
6. C. K. Barrett: *The First Epistle to the Corinthians* (Adam and Charles Black, 1968), p.63-64.
7. J. I. Packer: *Fundamentalism and the Word of God* (Inter-Varsity Fellowship, 1958), p.137-138.

Kenneth Prior is an Anglican who has spent all of his ministry in local churches. At the same time he has had many interdenominational interests and devoted much time during his earlier years in student work, visiting Christian Unions, speaking at conferences and conducting university missions. He was for four years President of the Evangelical Alliance of which he is now an active vice-president. He is married to Dorothy and they have two grown-up daughters and a son, and two grandchildren. He has written *God and Mammon* (Hodder and Stoughton and Westminster Press, 1965), *The Way of Holiness* (IVP, UK and USA, 1967 and Christian Focus, 1994) and *The Perils of Leadership* (IVP, USA, 1989). He is now in active retirement and living in North London. He preaches every Sunday in churches of various denominations.